# YOU CAN
## *read music*

### by Amy Appleby

*To Alison Marie Earley, for her inspiration*

Copyright © 1990, 1995 by Amsco Publications,
A Division of Music Sales Corporation, New York, NY.

Order No. AM 932327
US International Standard Book Number: 0.8256.1514.3
UK International Standard Book Number: 0.7119.5212.4

*Exclusive Distributors:*
**Music Sales Corporation**
257 Park Avenue South, New York, NY 10010 USA
**Music Sales Limited**
8/9 Frith Street, London W1V 5TZ England
**Music Sales Pty. Limited**
120 Rothschild Street, Rosebery, Sydney, NSW 2018, Australia

Printed and bound in the United States of America by
Vicks Lithograph and Printing

**Amsco Publications**
*New York • London • Paris • Sydney*

# Compact Disc Track Listing

| track | page | |
|---|---|---|
| 1 | 1 | **Introduction** |
| 2 | 2 | **The Treble Clef** |
| 3 | 4 | *Yankee Doodle* |
| 4 | | Leger Lines in Treble Clef |
| 5 | | *Aura Lee* |
| 6 | 5 | *Surprise Symphony* |
| 7 | | *Angels We Have Heard on High* |
| 8 | | *Scarborough Fair* |
| 9 | | Playing Notes in Treble Clef |
| 10 | 6 | *Twinkle, Twinkle, Little Star/My Bonnie* |
| 11 | 7 | **The Bass Clef** |
| 12 | 8 | *Danny Boy* |
| 13 | 9 | Leger Lines in Bass Clef |
| 14 | | *Hark! the Herald Angels Sing* |
| 15 | | *Westminister Chimes* |
| 16 | | *The Ashgrove* |
| 17 | 10 | Playing Notes in Bass Clef |
| 18 | | *Frère Jacques* |
| 19 | 11 | *God Rest Ye Merry, Gentlemen* |
| 20 | | *Ode to Joy* |
| 21 | | **Notes in the Treble and Bass Clefs** |
| 22 | 13 | *Old MacDonald* |
| 23 | | *Camptown Races* |
| 24 | | *The Streets of Loredo* |
| 25 | | *Good King Wenceslas* |
| 26 | 14 | *The Band Played On* |
| 27 | | *Jesu, Joy of Man's Desiring* |
| 28 | | The Octave Sign |
| 29 | 16 | **Note Values and Rhythm** |
| 30 | 18 | **Reading a Song Melody: Pitch and Rhythm/***Jingle Bells* |
| 31 | | Rests |
| 32 | 19 | Pickup Notes/*Polly-Wolly Doodle* |
| 33 | 20 | Dotted Notes and Rests |
| 34 | 21 | *I've Been Working on the Railroad* |
| 35 | 22 | **Time Signatures/**4/4 Time |
| 36 | 23 | 3/4 Time/*Drink to Me Only With Thine Eyes* |
| 37 | 24 | 2/4 Time/*Wedding March* |
| 38 | | 2/2 Time/*Turkey in the Straw* |
| 39 | 25 | 2/8, 3/8, and 4/8 Time |
| 40 | 26 | **Accidentals** |
| 41 | 29 | *Show Me the Way to Go Home* |
| 42 | | *Für Elise* |
| 43 | | *Shine On Harvest Moon* |
| 44 | | *I Don't Want to Walk Without You Baby* |
| 45 | 30 | **Major Key Signatures and Scales/**The Key of C Major |
| 46 | | The Sharp Keys |
| 47 | 34 | The Flat Keys |
| 48 | 37 | **Compound Time Signatures** |
| 49 | 38 | *Sweet Betsy From Pike* |
| 50 | 39 | *Boogie-Woogie Bugle Boy* |
| 51 | | *Barcarolle* |
| 52 | | *Beautiful Dreamer* |
| 53 | 40 | **More About Note Values and Rhythm** |
| 54 | 42 | Triplets and Other Note Groupings |
| 55 | 46 | **Dynamics** |
| 56 | 50 | **Accents and Articulations** |
| 57 | 52 | **Ornaments/**Grace Note |
| 58 | 53 | Trill |
| 59 | | Tremolo |
| 60 | 54 | Turns |
| 61 | 55 | Mordents |
| 62 | 56 | **Intervals/**Diatonic Intervals |
| 63 | 57 | Chromatic Intervals |
| 64 | 60 | Melodic Interval Examples |
| 65 | 61 | **Double Sharps and Flats** |
| 66 | 63 | **Minor Key Signatures and Scales** |
| 67 | 68 | **Introduction to Chords** |
| 68 | 69 | Inversions |
| 69 | | Seventh Chord |
| 70 | 70 | Minor Chords |
| 71 | | Minor Seventh Chord |
| 72 | 71 | Augmented and Diminished Chords |
| 73 | | Major Sixth and Major Seventh Chords |
| 74 | 80 | Reading a Lead Sheet/*Aura Lee* |
| 75 | 81 | *Danny Boy* |

# Table of Contents

Introduction       1
Reading Notes on the Staff       2
  The Treble Clef       2
    Naming Notes       2
    Notes on the Staff       3
    Leger Lines       4
    Playing Notes       5
  The Bass Clef       7
    Leger Lines       9
    Playing Notes       10
  Notes in the Treble and Bass Clefs       11
    The Grand Staff       14
    The Octave Sign       14
Note Values and Rhythm       16
  Reading a Song Melody: Pitch and Rhythm       18
  Rests       18
  Pickup Notes       19
  Dotted Notes and Rests       20
Time Signatures       22
  $\frac{4}{4}$ Time       22
  $\frac{3}{4}$ Time       23
  $\frac{2}{4}$ Time       24
  $\frac{2}{2}$ Time       24
  $\frac{3}{2}$ and $\frac{4}{2}$ Time       25
  $\frac{2}{8}$, $\frac{3}{8}$, and $\frac{4}{8}$ Time       25
Accidentals       26
  Sharps       26
  Flats       27
  Naturals       28
Major Key Signatures and Scales       30
  The Key of C Major       30
  The Sharp Keys       30
  The Flat Keys       34
Compound Time Signatures       37
More About Note Values and Rhythm       40
  Ties       40
  Extended Rests       41
  Pauses       41
  Triplets and Other Note Groupings       42

Tempo 44
    Metronome Markings 44
Expression 45
Dynamics 46
Structure 47
    Repeat Sign 47
    Repeat Markings: Da Capo and Dal Segno 48
    Alternate Endings 48
Accents and Articulations 50
    Staccato 50
    Accents 50
    Slur 51
    Phrase Mark 51
Ornaments 52
    Grace Note 52
    Trill 53
    Tremolo 53
    Turns 54
    Mordents 55
Intervals 56
    Diatonic Intervals 56
    Chromatic Intervals 57
Double Sharps and Double Flats 61
Minor Key Signatures and Scales 63
Introduction to Chords 68
    Major Chord 68
    Inversions 69
    Seventh Chord 69
    Minor Chord 70
    Minor Seventh Chord 70
    Augmented and Diminished Chords 71
    Major Sixth and Major Seventh Chords 71
    Basic Chords in All Keys 71
    Reading a Lead Sheet 80
    Transposing Chords 80
    Further Chord Study 82

# Introduction

It's true. With a little study and practice, anyone can read music! No matter what kind of instrument you play, or what style of music you prefer, this book will provide you with everything you need to know to read music—and to communicate effectively with other musicians and composers about standard music notation. By following this proven, step-by-step method, you can quickly master the basics of sight-reading—from the fundamentals of melody, harmony, and rhythm to the subtleties of musical expression and ornamentation.

Learning to read music need not be a dull process of memorizing rules. In fact, you'll find many musical concepts quite easy to understand when you see and hear how they function in familiar songs. That's why this learning method includes a wide range of music—from classical, blues, and pop to some best-loved traditional favorites. You'll also find special exercises to help you sharpen your new-found skills. These give you a chance to test your ability to read and understand music at each important stage in the learning process.

Whether you are an instrumentalist, singer, or composer, if you want to expand your understanding and mastery of music, you can make a giant leap forward by learning to read it from the printed page. It's true that a few composers and artists—from Irving Berlin and Ezio Pinza to some of today's best-loved rock and pop stars—have made it big without ever learning to read a note. Still, countless more professionals will tell you that learning to read music is the biggest break they've ever had. The wonderful thing is that this big break doesn't come from a recording company or producer—it is a musical gift that you give to yourself.

# Reading Notes on the Staff

Written music is a universal language of notes and symbols, arranged on the musical *staff*, which consists of five lines and four spaces, as shown.

## The Treble Clef

Before you can read or write notes on the staff, you must first determine which clef is appropriate, given the musical context. *Clefs* are symbols that provide a frame of reference for writing notes on the staff. In other words, the clef tells the musician exactly which tones are indicated by the notes occurring on each line and space of the staff.

There are two clefs that commonly appear in written music: the treble clef and the bass clef. The *treble clef* is usually used in music intended for middle- and high-range instruments and voices, while the *bass clef* is used in music written for lower instruments and voices. Let's take a look at the treble clef on the staff.

This clef is also sometimes called the *G clef* because the curlicue of the clef sign circles the second line up from the bottom of the staff. This line marks the position of the G note, and so provides a frame of reference for notes placed on any of the other lines and spaces of the staff. Notes that appear on a staff with a treble clef at the beginning are said to be written "in the treble clef."

### Naming Notes

*Notes* are the building blocks of music. Each note usually indicates two qualities: pitch and duration. *Pitch* is simply how high or low a particular tone sounds. *Duration* is how long an individual tone should last. We'll get into note duration in the next chapter. For now, let's focus on how notes indicate pitch.

Musical notes are named using the first seven letters of the alphabet: A, B, C, D, E, F, and G. These letter names indicate notes in an ascending sequence—from low to high. After the final G note, the sequence begins again: A, B, C, D, E, F, G, A, B, C, D, E, F, G, and so on. Most instruments are able to produce a large enough range of notes to repeat this seven-note sequence several times.

The distance between any two notes with the same letter name is called an *octave*. This term, from the Greek word meaning "eight," reminds us that the notes' letter names repeat at every eighth tone of the sequence. Although the two tones that form an octave are actually different notes (one being lower than the other)—they bear a strong resemblance to one another. Each tone sounds as if it were just a higher or lower version of the same note. Thus, an A note is closely related to the A note above it. The same relationship occurs for all B notes, C notes, and so on, respectively.

## Notes on the Staff

Here are some notes arranged on the staff in the treble clef. Notice that a note falls on every line and space of the staff. When notes are arranged in a sequence like this they are collectively called a *scale*.

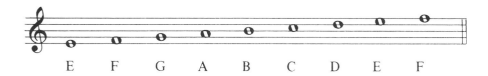

Take the time to memorize the position and name of each of these notes. You may find it helpful to learn the notes that fall on lines separately from those that occur in the spaces of the staff. Many music teachers recommend using this mnemonic phrase for memorizing the notes that occur on the lines of a staff in the treble clef.

You may want to make up your own phrase to use for memorizing these notes—like "**E**ggs **G**o **B**ad **D**uring **F**ebruary" or "**E**ach **G**reat **B**allplayer **D**rinks **F**luids." Once you choose the phrase that will work best for you—stick to it. This should help you to get these notes firmly set in your mind. As you become more and more adept at reading music, you will be able to drop this mnemonic tool and begin to recognize individual notes solely by their placement on the staff.

Now let's look at the notes that fall in the spaces of the staff.

The obvious way to memorize these notes is to remember that they spell the word "face" when read from the bottom up. Again, you should be able to drop this association very soon and recognize the notes on their own.

Now test your ability to identify notes by looking at the familiar folk tune "Yankee Doodle." Write the appropriate letter name in the space provided below each note. Don't be confused by the fact that some notes are filled in while others are not, or that some have stems, dots, or flags, while others do not. We will discuss these different *note values* in the section on rhythm that follows. You only need to see where the circular portion of the note (or *notehead*) falls to determine the note name.

**Yankee Doodle**

## Leger Lines

Now that you are familiar with the notes on the staff in the treble clef, let's take a look at the notes that extend above and below the staff. The additional lines used to extend notes beyond the staff in this way are referred to as *leger lines*.

Take the time to memorize the position and names of each of these new notes. Then label each of the notes in the familiar tune phrases provided below. (Again, don't be confused by the dots and stems.)

**Aura Lee** *(Love Me Tender)*

**Surprise Symphony**

**Angels We Have Heard on High**

**Scarborough Fair**

## Playing Notes

As mentioned previously, reading music is a practical skill, and should be directly related to the development of your musical ear. Whether you are a singer, composer, or instrumentalist, it is very helpful to know how notes sound and where they are located on the piano. Here's how the notes you have learned in the treble clef correspond to the white keys of the piano. The note labeled *Middle C* is the C note nearest to the center of the keyboard.

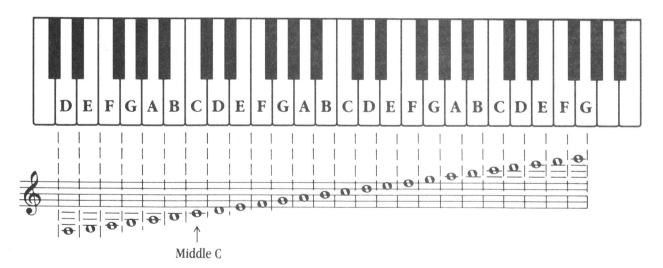

Middle C

The *black notes* of the piano occur in groups of two and three. The white key which occurs before every group of two black notes is a C note. The white key which occurs before every group of three black notes is an F note.

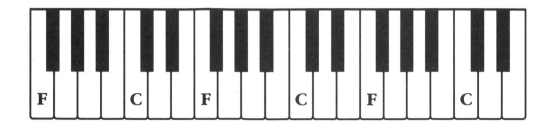

You can see that the black notes provide a frame of reference for memorizing all of the white keys on the piano keyboard; that is, a D note occurs in the middle of every group of two black keys, the E note occurs immediately after every group of two black keys, and so on. We'll discuss the black keys in more detail when we get into *sharps* and *flats*. For now, take the time to memorize the letter names of the white keys of the piano keyboard.

Once you know the white keys by heart, find yourself a piano (or any other keyboard instrument), and play these two familiar melody phrases. Play the notes slowly and evenly, and let the last note of each melody phrase last an extra beat. If you are a soprano or alto—or male singer with a workable extra-high range (called *falsetto*)—sing the letter name of each note as you play these phrases on the piano.

**Twinkle, Twinkle, Little Star**

**My Bonnie**

Perhaps you play another type of instrument that commonly uses the treble clef—like the violin, flute, clarinet, or guitar. If so, you should first memorize the playing position of the notes you have just learned for your particular instrument, and then play the melody phrases again on that instrument. (You'll need to get a fingering chart for your instrument to learn how to play these notes.)

Certain instruments—like the clarinet, trumpet, and saxophone—sound lower or higher than the notes written on staff. These are called *transposing instruments*. Guitarists should be aware that guitar music is written an octave higher than it actually sounds when played. Here is a guitar fingering chart for a range of notes in the treble clef.

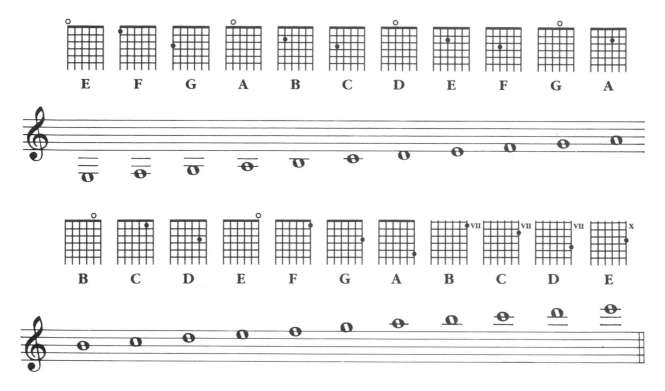

If you find that any of the exercises in this book require you to play notes that are outside the range of your particular instrument or voice, you can substitute the nearest note of the same letter that is within your range. If a note is too high for your instrument or voice, drop down an octave to the note of the same letter name. If a note is too low, play or sing that note an octave higher.

For more practice playing notes in treble clef, turn back to "Yankee Doodle" and play it on the piano— or use the treble instrument of your choice to play the tune. Again, singers with a treble range should play the tune on the piano while singing the letter name of each note.

## The Bass Clef

Now that you are familiar with reading and playing notes in the treble clef, let's take a look at the notes in the bass clef. As mentioned earlier, the *bass clef* is used for writing music for low instruments and voices. This clef is also sometimes called the *F clef* because it forms a curlicue on the fourth line up from the bottom of the staff. The two small dots of the clef further emphasize this line. In this way, the clef indicates the position of the F note as a reference point for notes placed on any other lines and spaces of the staff.

Here are the notes arranged on the staff in the bass clef. Just as in treble clef, here a note falls on every line and space of the staff. As you know, when notes are arranged in a sequence like this they are collectively called a *scale*.

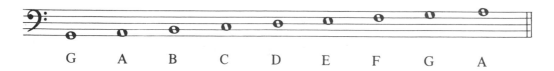

Take the time to memorize the position and name of each of these bass clef notes. Here again, you may find it helpful to learn the notes that fall on lines separately from those that occur in the spaces of the staff. Here's a useful mnemonic phrase for memorizing the bass clef notes that occur on the lines of the staff.

Great    Big    Dreams For    America

Feel free to make up your own phrase to remember these notes. Just remember that this is only a learning device. With a little practice, you should be able to recognize these notes by their placement on the staff. Now look at the notes that fall in the spaces of a staff that features a bass clef. The time-honored phrase used for remembering these notes is "**All Cows Eat Grass**."

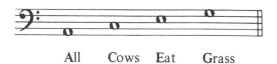

All    Cows    Eat    Grass

Once you feel you know the note names for the lines and spaces of the staff, test your ability to identify these notes by looking at the opening phrase of some well-known tunes. Write in the appropriate letter name in the space provided below each note of this version of "Danny Boy," also known as "Londonderry Air." The zigzag symbol at the beginning of measures 1, 5, 9, and 13 is a *rest,* or pause. You'll learn all about rests later on.

**Danny Boy** *(Londonderry Air)*

## Leger Lines

Now that you are familiar with the notes on the staff in the bass clef, let's take a look at the notes that extend above and below the staff. As in treble clef, leger lines are used here to extend notes beyond the staff.

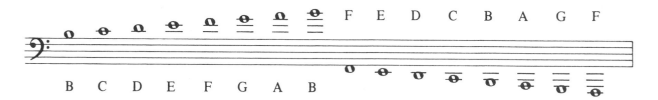

Take the time to memorize the position and name of each of these new notes. Then label each of the notes in the popular tune fragments provided below.

### Hark! the Herald Angels Sing

### Westminister Chimes

### The Ashgrove

## Playing Notes

Now let's examine the notes you have just learned in the bass clef as they correspond to the white keys of the piano.

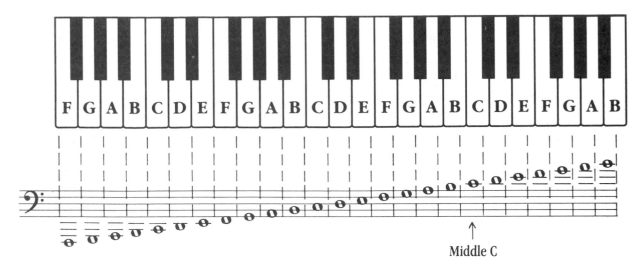

Take the time to memorize the position and name of each of these new notes as they appear on the staff. Since the treble clef notes that extend below the staff overlap quite a bit with these bass clef notes, you actually only have a few new key positions to memorize on the keyboard, as shown below. (Notice the position of the C note below Middle C in this diagram.)

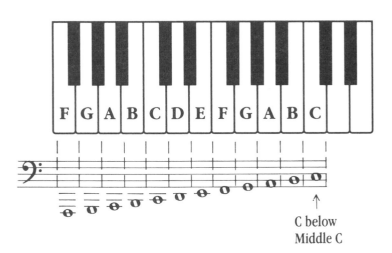

Once you feel you know the bass clef notes, find yourself a piano, and play the following melody phrases. You may want to try playing these tunes with your left hand, since pianists usually play notes in bass clef with this hand. If you are a baritone or bass singer, sing the letter name of each note of these phrases as you play them on the piano.

### Frère Jacques

---

**God Rest Ye Merry, Gentlemen**

If you play an instrument that commonly uses the bass clef—like the trombone, string bass, bassoon, or tuba—you need to be quite familiar with the notes in bass clef. Memorize the playing position of the notes you have just learned for your particular instrument, and then play the melody phrases. Here again, you'll need a fingering chart for your instrument to learn how to play these notes.

For more practice playing notes in bass clef, play Beethoven's "Ode to Joy" on the piano—or use the bass instrument of your choice to play this tune. Again, singers with a bass range should play the tune on the piano while singing the letter name of each note.

**Ode to Joy**

# Notes in the Treble and Bass Clefs

As mentioned earlier, there is significant overlap of the notes you have learned in the treble clef and bass clef, respectively. To see this overlap, let's look at the notes of both clefs together in relation to the keys of the piano.

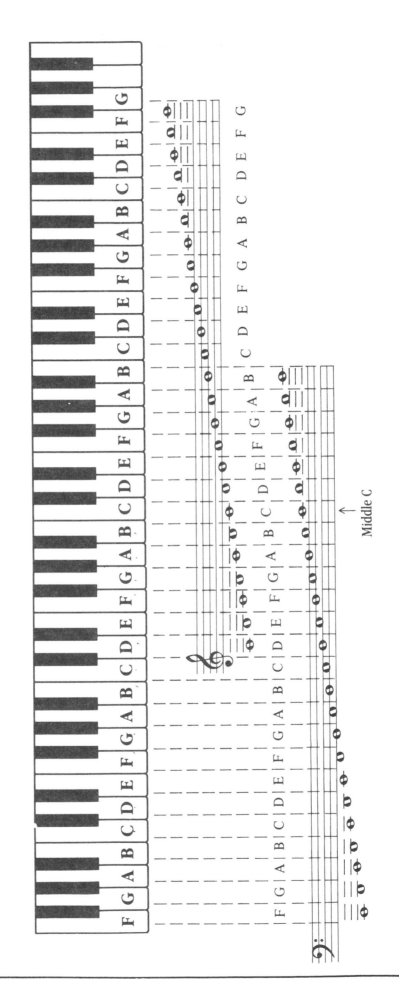

You can see that many bass clef notes correspond to exactly the same keys as treble clef notes. Corresponding notes only look different because they are written in their respective clefs—they sound exactly the same. Let's eliminate the overlapping notes between clefs, and view the notes on both staves taken together.

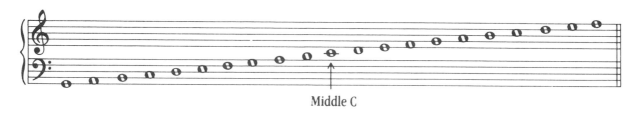

Middle C

Notice that there is only one leger line between the staves. This line indicates the position for Middle C (which is the C note nearest the center of your keyboard).

Let's test your ability to identify notes in both the treble and bass clefs. Supply the letter names for the notes in the familiar melody phrases that follow. Be sure to pay attention to the clef signs.

**Old MacDonald**

____  ____  ____  ____  ____  ____  ____

**Camptown Races**

____  ____  ____  ____  ____  ____  ____  ____

**The Streets of Laredo**

____  ____  ____  ____  ____  ____  ____  ____  ____  ____  ____

**Good King Wenceslas**

____  ____  ____  ____  ____  ____  ____

**The Band Played On**

**Jesu, Joy of Man's Desiring**

Now try playing these melodies on the piano, or on the instrument of your choice. If the music for the instrument you use is commonly written in the treble clef, you only need to play the first three melody phrases. If the music for the instrument you use is commonly notated in bass clef, play only the last three melody phrases. Soprano and alto singers only need to sing the first three melody phrases. Tenor and bass singers should stick to the last three phrases. As before, sing the name of each note as you play the phrases on the piano or guitar.

## The Grand Staff

Pianists, in particular, should be quite familiar with the note names in both clefs. This is because music for piano is written on the *grand staff,* which is actually two staves joined together.

The staff with the treble clef is used to indicate music to be played by the right hand. The bass clef staff governs the left hand. The bracket which links the two staves together is called a *brace.*

## The Octave Sign

Sometimes a composer or arranger intends for a passage to be played an octave higher than the notes shown on the staff. In treble clef, these passages are marked by an *octave sign* (a dotted line with **8va, 8,** or **8ve**) above the staff.

Written Notes       Actual Notes Played

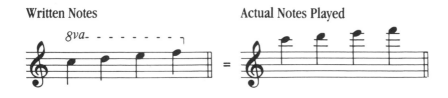

When an octave sign appears below the staff, the indicated passage should be played an octave lower than written. This inverted octave sign is only used to mark passages in bass clef (which are sometimes also marked with the Italian word *bassa*).

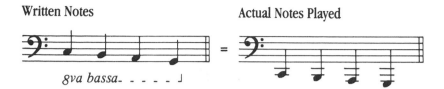

Written Notes           Actual Notes Played

Octave signs are generally used to write very high passages in treble clef or very low passages in bass clef without using too many leger lines. This makes the music easier to read.

You should now be quite familiar with reading and hearing the notes in the treble and bass clefs. Now let's take a look at how different kinds of notes indicate rhythm.

# Note Values and Rhythm

As you have learned, the position of the note on the staff indicates a particular *pitch* (that is, how high or low a note sounds). Each note also has a *note value,* or *duration,* (that is, how long the note should last). The duration of a note is counted in *beats.* Here are the basic note shapes and their usual durations. Take the time to memorize the appearance and value of each of these notes.

◦ A **whole note** lasts for four beats.

♩ A **half note** lasts for two beats.

♩ A **quarter note** lasts for one beat.

♪ An **eighth note** lasts for one-half of a beat.

♪ A **sixteenth note** lasts for one-fourth of a beat.

♪ A **thirty-second note** lasts for one-eighth of a beat.

An eighth note has three components. The circular portion of the note is called the *notehead,* the line is called the *stem,* and the tail is called the *flag.*

←Flag
←Stem
←Head

The flag of the sixteenth note is made with two lines, while the thirty-second-note flag is made of three lines. Groups of consecutive eighth, sixteenth, and thirty-second notes are often linked with *beams,* as shown.

Eighth Notes          Sixteenth Notes          Thirty-second Notes

Stem direction is determined by a note's placement on the staff. In either clef, notes occurring below the middle line of the staff have stems that point upward. Notes that occur on or above the middle line should have downward stems. Although this is the preferable rule regarding stem direction, some printed music features notes on the middle line with upward stems. These occur only when other notes in the same measure feature upward stems. Notes connected by a beam should always feature the same stem direction (as determined by the natural stem direction of the majority of notes in the group).

Compare the different notes you have learned and their relative values.

| | | |
|---|---|---|
| Whole Note: | | |
| Half Note: | | |
| Quarter Note: | | |
| Eighth Note: | | |
| Sixteenth Note: | | |
| Thirty-second Note: | | |

As you can see, two half-notes equal the duration of one whole-note, four quarter-notes equal the duration of one whole-note, eight eighth-notes equal the duration of one whole-note, and so on.

In order to make it easy to count the rhythm of written music, the staff is divided into sections called *measures,* or *bars*. The vertical lines that divide the staff in this way are called *barlines*. A *double barline* is used to indicate the end of a piece of music. (A lighter double barline is used to divide important sections of a piece.)

Take a look at some of the different note values in measures on the staff. Each measure in this example contains four beats. Count the beats of each measure aloud slowly and evenly while you clap the rhythm indicated by the notes.

**Count:** 1 2 3 4   1 2 3 4   1 2 3 4   1 and 2 and 3 and 4 and

The next example combines notes of different durations in each measure. Count the beats aloud as you clap the indicated rhythm. Again, be sure to count slowly and evenly without halting.

**Count:** 1 2 3 4   1 2 and 3 4   1 and 2 and 3 4   1 and 2 3 4

# Reading a Song Melody: Pitch and Rhythm

Now that you are familiar with these basic note values, get ready to combine your knowledge of pitch and rhythm to read a familiar song melody. First count and clap the rhythm of "Jingle Bells," as you did for the previous two exercises. Then play the song on the piano, sing it, or use another instrument to play this melody. Be sure you play it slowly and evenly without halting.

**Jingle Bells**

Once you are comfortable playing "Jingle Bells" at a slow speed, try playing it at a medium-fast speed. The technical term for speed in music is *tempo*. Even at this faster tempo, every beat of the song should still be steady and clear.

# Rests

Music is usually composed of sounds and silences. The silent beats in music are represented by signs called *rests*. Rests are named and valued in correspondence with the note values you learned in the previous section.

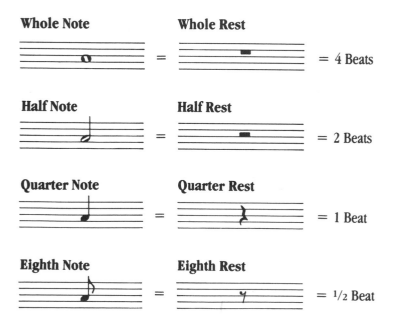

| **Sixteenth Note** | | **Sixteenth Rest** | |
|---|---|---|---|

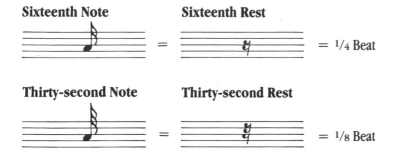

$= \frac{1}{4}$ Beat

$= \frac{1}{8}$ Beat

Rests and notes may be combined in the same measure, as long as their combined values add up to the correct number of beats (in this example, four beats to a measure). Count the beats of this phrase as you clap the rhythm of the notes.

**Count:**  1  2  3  4  |  1  2  3  4  |  1  and  2  3  and  4  |  1  and  2  and  3  and  4  and

Count the beats of this next phrase as you clap the rhythm of the notes. Then play (or sing and play) this melody slowly and evenly.

**Count:**  1  2  3  4  |  1  2  3  4  |  1  2  and  3  and  4  and  |  1  2  3  4

# Pickup Notes

Certain song melodies require an incomplete first measure to provide for a *pickup,* which is simply a note or notes that occur before the first stressed beat of the song. When a musical composition features a partial measure containing a pickup, it usually makes up the remaining beats of the first measure in the last measure of the piece. This means that the last measure of the piece will also be incomplete. You can see how this works in "Polly-Wolly Doodle."

**Polly-Wolly Doodle**

**Count:**  4  and  |  1  2  3  4  and  |  1  2  3  4  |  1  and  2  and  3  and  4  and  |  1  2  3

Now let's move on to some more complex note and rest values.

# Dotted Notes and Rests

A dot placed after any note or rest means that it should last one-and-a-half times its normal duration. For example, if you add a dot after a half note (which normally lasts two beats), you get a *dotted half note,* which has a duration of three beats.

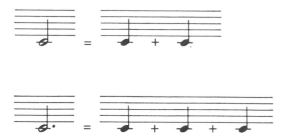

In the same way, if you add a dot to a quarter rest, you get a *dotted quarter rest,* which indicates a silence of one-and-a-half beats.

It's easy to understand dotted notes and rests when you compare them with the regular note and rest values you have already learned.

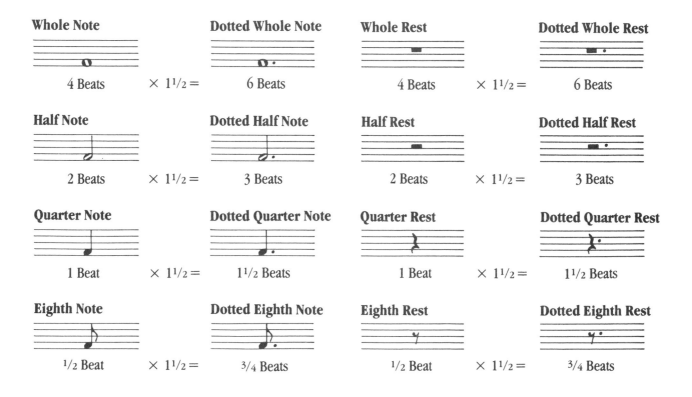

| Whole Note | | Dotted Whole Note | Whole Rest | | Dotted Whole Rest |
|---|---|---|---|---|---|
| 4 Beats | × 1½ = | 6 Beats | 4 Beats | × 1½ = | 6 Beats |

| Half Note | | Dotted Half Note | Half Rest | | Dotted Half Rest |
|---|---|---|---|---|---|
| 2 Beats | × 1½ = | 3 Beats | 2 Beats | × 1½ = | 3 Beats |

| Quarter Note | | Dotted Quarter Note | Quarter Rest | | Dotted Quarter Rest |
|---|---|---|---|---|---|
| 1 Beat | × 1½ = | 1½ Beats | 1 Beat | × 1½ = | 1½ Beats |

| Eighth Note | | Dotted Eighth Note | Eighth Rest | | Dotted Eighth Rest |
|---|---|---|---|---|---|
| ½ Beat | × 1½ = | 3/4 Beats | ½ Beat | × 1½ = | 3/4 Beats |

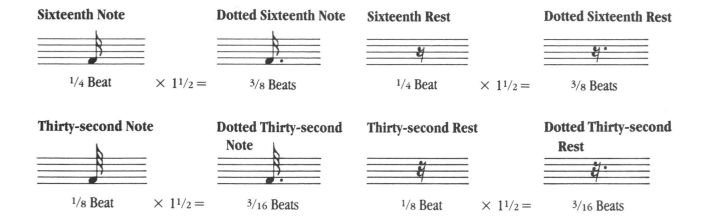

| Sixteenth Note | Dotted Sixteenth Note | Sixteenth Rest | Dotted Sixteenth Rest |
|---|---|---|---|
| 1/4 Beat    × 1 1/2 = | 3/8 Beats | 1/4 Beat    × 1 1/2 = | 3/8 Beats |

| Thirty-second Note | Dotted Thirty-second Note | Thirty-second Rest | Dotted Thirty-second Rest |
|---|---|---|---|
| 1/8 Beat    × 1 1/2 = | 3/16 Beats | 1/8 Beat    × 1 1/2 = | 3/16 Beats |

Take the time to memorize the appearance and value of each dotted note and rest. Then count the beats in the next example as you clap the rhythm indicated by the notes. (Notice how the dotted eighth notes are connected by beams to the sixteenth notes in the third measure.)

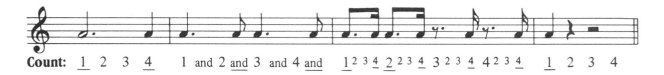

**Count:** 1  2  3  4     1  and  2  and  3  and  4  and     1 2 3 4  2 2 3 4  3 2 3 4  4 2 3 4     1  2  3  4

Now combine your knowledge of pitch and rhythm as you play (or play and sing) the opening phrase of "I've Been Working on the Railroad."

### I've Been Working on the Railroad

You may also encounter a *double dotted note* in written music. Two dots indicate that the note is worth one and three-fourths of its normal value. In this way, a double dotted whole note lasts for seven beats. A double dotted half note lasts for three-and-a-half beats.

𝅗𝅥 = 𝅘𝅥 + 𝅘𝅥

𝅗𝅥. = 𝅘𝅥 + 𝅘𝅥

𝅗𝅥.. = 𝅘𝅥 + 𝅘𝅥 + 𝅘𝅥𝅮

At this point, you should feel familiar with basic note and rest values, and how they function together in a piece of music. Let's move on to an overall discussion of musical rhythms and explore time signatures.

# Time Signatures

Every musical composition has a *time signature* at the beginning of the first staff. This symbol indicates two important facts about the overall rhythm of the piece.

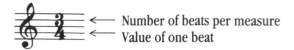 ← Number of beats per measure
← Value of one beat

The top number of the time signature indicates how many beats there are in each measure. The bottom number determines which type of note is worth one beat.

**2** = Half Note
**4** = Quarter Note
**8** = Eighth Note

The time signature is a guidepost to the overall rhythm of a piece of music. Each time signature has a characteristic pattern of stressed and unstressed beats. A composer or arranger chooses the time signature which best matches the natural stresses of a particular piece or section of music.

In the sections that follow, you'll take a look at some basic time signatures and their characteristic patterns of stress.

## $\frac{4}{4}$ Time

$\frac{4}{4}$ (pronounced "four-four") is the most common time signature used in written music. Much of the music we've examined in the book so far has been in $\frac{4}{4}$ time—that is, with four beats in each measure and the quarter note lasting for its natural value of one beat.

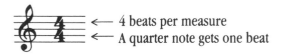 ← 4 beats per measure
← A quarter note gets one beat

The $\frac{4}{4}$ time signature is so prevalent that it is sometimes referred to as "common time" and notated with this shorthand symbol.

Each time signature has a natural, characteristic pattern of stressed and unstressed beats. The first beat of each measure in any time signature receives the most stress. In $\frac{4}{4}$ time, the third beat is also stressed, but to a lesser extent.

**Stress**   Stress

"Jingle Bells" provides a strong example of the natural stresses which occur in $\frac{4}{4}$ time. (The stressed beats are indicated with boldface numbers.)

**Jingle Bells**

1 2 3 4 1 2 3 4 1 2 3 4 1 2 3 4

# $\frac{3}{4}$ Time

$\frac{3}{4}$ (or "three-four") time is also sometimes called *waltz time*, since this is the characteristic time signature of this dance form. However, there are many other types of compositions that employ this time signature. In $\frac{3}{4}$ time, the quarter note still receives its normal value, but there are only three beats in every measure.

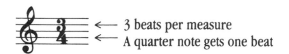
← 3 beats per measure
← A quarter note gets one beat

The natural stress of $\frac{3}{4}$ time falls on the first beat of each measure only. Sing or hum the first phrase of "Drink to Me Only With Thine Eyes" to get a feeling for the natural, lilting stress of $\frac{3}{4}$ time.

**Drink to Me Only With Thine Eyes**

1 2 3 1 2 3 1 2 3 1 2 3

1 2 3 1 2 3 1 2 3

# $\frac{2}{4}$ Time

$\frac{2}{4}$ time calls for only two beats in each measure with a stress on every other beat. Richard Wagner's familiar "Wedding March" illustrates the strong and regular stress pattern of this time signature. Notice the bass clef.

**Wedding March**

# $\frac{2}{2}$ Time

So far, we've looked at time signatures that call for the quarter note to receive its natural value of one beat. $\frac{2}{2}$ time, or *cut time*, indicates that a half note lasts for only one beat—with two beats in each measure. $\frac{2}{2}$ time is usually noted with this shorthand symbol ($\mathcal{C}$). This time signature makes it easier for musicians to read music with many short note values or complex rhythms. Here's the traditional fiddle tune "Turkey in the Straw" in $\frac{2}{2}$ time. Notice that the stresses fall on every other beat.

**Turkey in the Straw**

Take a look at how much more difficult this song is to read when notated in $\frac{2}{4}$ time. The sixteenth notes seem harder to count at a glance than the eighth notes in the above example.

**Turkey in the Straw**

# $\frac{3}{2}$ and $\frac{4}{2}$ Time

$\frac{3}{2}$ and $\frac{4}{2}$ time signatures also call for the half note to equal one beat.

# $\frac{2}{8}$, $\frac{3}{8}$, and $\frac{4}{8}$ Time

Some time signatures call for an eighth note to be valued as one beat. Try counting aloud as you clap the rhythm of these phrases. (Stressed beats are indicated with boldface numbers.)

All of the time signatures we've looked at so far are called *simple time signatures* because they require a basic arrangement of the number of beats in each measure and the value of each beat. *Compound time signatures* will be discussed in a later section.

# Accidentals

Until this point in your study of written music, all of the musical examples provided have contained no sharps or flats. You have become quite familiar with those notes represented by the white keys of the piano: A, B, C, D, E, F, and G. As you may have already noticed, the black keys of the piano keyboard provide pitches in between these notes. These pitches are collectively called *accidentals*. They are more commonly called *sharp* or *flat notes,* depending on their musical context. The names of these notes are formed by adding a *sharp sign* (♯) or *flat sign* (♭) after the note letter name. These signs, as well as the notes themselves, are often simply called *sharps* and *flats.*

## Sharps

Let's take a look at the sharp notes as they relate to a portion of the piano keyboard.

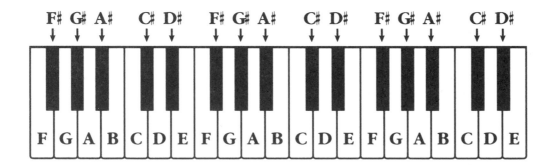

As you can see, each sharp key occurs just above the white key with the same letter name. Thus, the black note in between the C and D notes is labeled *C♯,* the black note in between the D and E keys is *D♯,* and so on. Notice that no sharp occurs between the E and F keys, or between the B and C keys. Here's the complete sequence of natural and sharp note names.

A - A♯ - B - C - C♯ - D - D♯ - E - F - F♯ - G - G♯ - A

The distance between each of these notes is called a *half step.* A sequence of half steps is called a *chromatic scale.* Let's take a look at the chromatic scale, beginning on Middle C, as notated on the staff in treble clef.

Here's the same scale in bass clef, an octave lower.

| C | C♯ | D | D♯ | E | F | F♯ | G | G♯ | A | A♯ | B | C |

Try playing these scales on the piano, or on the instrument of your choice. If you play an instrument other than the piano, refer to a note fingering chart to find out how to play each of these new notes. If you are a singer, practice singing the chromatic scale as you play along on the piano or guitar. Take the time to memorize the position and name of each of the sharp notes as they appear on the keyboard and staff.

# Flats

Sometimes the black keys of the piano are viewed as *flat notes* rather than sharp notes. The reason for having two names for each of these notes will be clear when we discuss *key signatures* in the next section. For now, let's get to know the names of the flat notes and then compare them to those of the sharp notes.

A flat note occurs one note lower than the white key of the same letter name on the piano keyboard. The flat sign appears after the letter name of the lowered white key to indicate the black-key name. Thus, the black-key note in between the C and D notes is labeled *D♭,* the black-key note in between the D and E keys is *E♭,* and so on. No flat occurs between the E and F keys, or between the B and C keys.

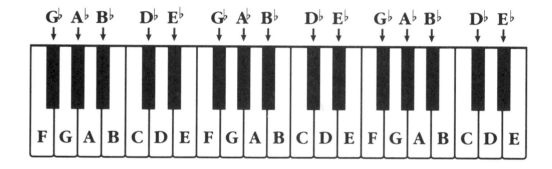

Here's the complete sequence of natural and flat note names.

A - B♭ - B - C - D♭ - D - E♭ - E - F - G♭ - G - A♭ - A

Let's take a look at how the chromatic scale is notated using flats in treble clef.

| C | B | B♭ | A | A♭ | G | G♭ | F | E | E♭ | D | D♭ | C |

Here's the same scale in bass clef, an octave lower.

C    B    B♭    A    A♭    G    G♭    F    E    E♭    D    D♭    C

Take the time to memorize the name and position of each of these flat notes as they appear on the keyboard and staff. Now play these scales on the piano—or play the appropriate scale on the treble or bass instrument of your choice.

Here's an important rule which applies to both sharps and flats: If a note appears with a sharp or flat sign, all subsequent notes in the same position on the staff of that measure are also affected by that sign.

A    A♯    A♯    A♯    A                A    A♭    A♭    A♭    A

As you can see in the two preceding examples, the barline cancels both sharp and flat signs.

## Naturals

A *natural sign* also cancels a sharp or flat sign that has appeared with a note of the same position. Because a barline cancels all flat and sharp signs, there's no need to use a natural sign unless you wish to cancel a flat or sharp that has already occurred in the same measure. Once a natural sign has been used, all other subsequent notes in the same position on the staff in that measure are affected by the natural sign.

A    A♯    A    A                A    A♭    A    A

As you might expect, a natural sign may be cancelled by a flat or sharp sign with a note of the same position in the same measure. (Notice that the barline then cancels the sharp.)

A    A♯    A    A♯    A

Some pieces contain both sharps and flats. Whether a note is flatted or sharped depends on its particular musical function in the piece. But, as a general rule, an accidental that leads up to a natural note is written as a sharp note—and an accidental that leads down to a natural note is written as a flat note. This rule is illustrated in "Melancholy Baby."

**Melancholy Baby**

Now test your ability to name musical notes by labeling each note with its appropriate letter name in the familiar tune phrases that follow. Be sure to take note of the clefs and time signatures—as well as the rules you have just learned for carrying over flats, sharps, and naturals in the same measure. (Notice that there is an "unnecessary" natural in the last measure of the first example. You will often see examples of such *courtesy accidentals*—sometimes enclosed in parentheses—included as an aid to the reader.)

**Show Me the Way to Go Home**

**Für Elise**

**Shine On Harvest Moon**

**I Don't Want to Walk Without You, Baby**

Give yourself some more practice at naming notes by examining other music in this way. Choose any piece of music and write down the names of each of the notes in sequence on a separate sheet of paper. If you encounter any musical symbols that you have not yet learned, just pass over them—we'll get to them in later sections of this book.

# Major Key Signatures and Scales

So far, we've looked at sharp, flat, and natural notes that are individually added to written music. These notes are called *accidentals* or *altered notes*. Many pieces of music require that certain notes be sharped or flatted as a general rule. The number of sharps or flats which occur regularly in a piece of music determines the *key*. Rather than writing in a sharp or flat sign every time one should occur, these signs are written in a *key signature* at the beginning of each staff.

Composers and arrangers place music in different keys to accommodate the needs of the particular ranges of the voices or instruments for which they are writing. Certain keys are easier to play on certain instruments. Using different keys for the individual sections or songs in a larger work—such as a symphony or a Broadway show—adds variety to a performance. This is important to remember if you are planning your own concert, or writing music for others to perform.

## The Key of C Major

Most of the musical examples in the book so far have been written in the *key of C major*, which has no sharps or flats. Thus, all the notes of the C major scale occur on the white keys of the piano keyboard. Once you understand the construction of the scale in the key of C major, you'll be able to build the scale and key signature for every other major key.

As you already know, the shortest distance between two notes is called a half step. A *whole step* is the equivalent of two half steps. Let's examine the pattern of whole steps and half steps in the C major scale.

**C Major Scale**

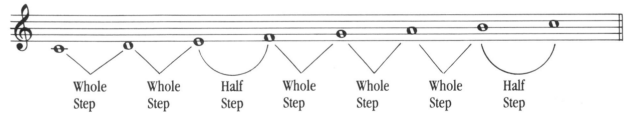

Take the time to memorize this important pattern, because it is the blueprint for all other major scales: whole step, whole step, half step, whole step, whole step, whole step, half step. If you play an instrument other than the piano, take the time to learn the fingering and sound of the notes of the C major scale on your instrument. Singers should sing this scale with piano or guitar accompaniment.

## The Sharp Keys

Once you are quite familiar with the step-by-step pattern of the C major scale, take a look at the *G major scale*. The notes of this scale are the building blocks for music in the *key of G major*. Notice that this scale requires an F♯ note in order to follow the proper step-by-step pattern for major scales.

**G Major Scale**

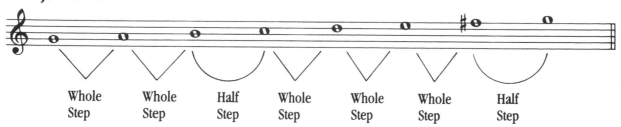

| Whole Step | Whole Step | Half Step | Whole Step | Whole Step | Whole Step | Half Step |

Since the F♯ note is a regular feature in the key of G major, it is represented in the key signature after the clef on every staff of the piece. This means that all notes which occur in the F position in the piece (unless otherwise marked) will be sharped—as in this excerpt from Schubert's "Unfinished Symphony."

**Theme From the Unfinished Symphony**

Keep in mind that the F♯ note indicated in the preceding key signature applies to all F♯ note positions in the piece, no matter how high or low. This applies to the bass clef as well.

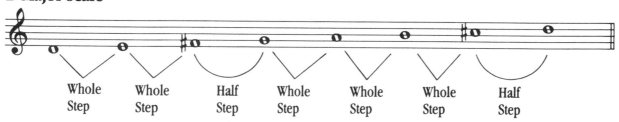

The *D major scale* follows the same step-by-step pattern as the C and G major scales.

**D Major Scale**

| Whole Step | Whole Step | Half Step | Whole Step | Whole Step | Whole Step | Half Step |

As you can see, this scale features two sharps. Its key signature is notated on the treble and bass staves as follows.

Let's take a look at all of the major key signatures and corresponding scales that contain sharps. Although it is not necessary to include any sharp signs next to the notes of these scales, they are shown here in parentheses for your reference.

**The Sharp Keys**

G Major Scale

D Major Scale

A Major Scale

E Major Scale

B Major Scale

F♯ Major Scale

C♯ Major Scale

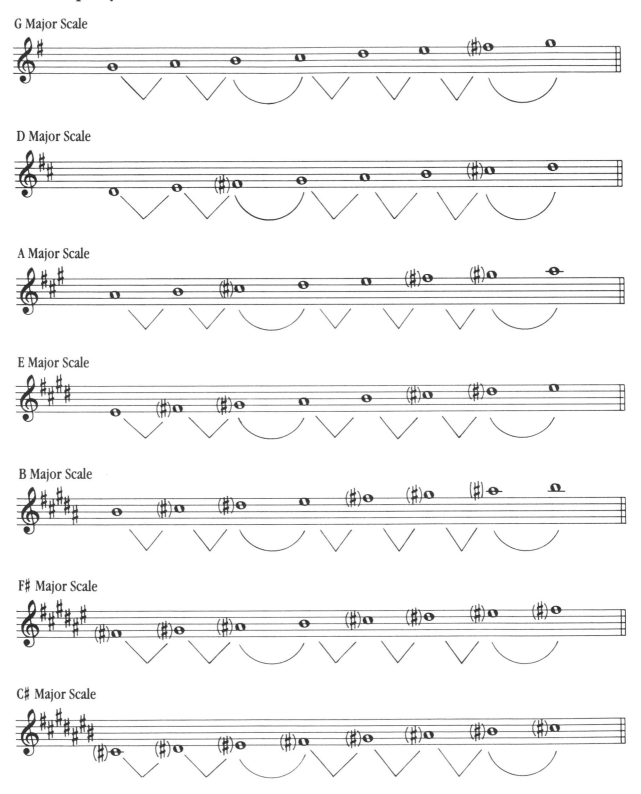

Here's a trick for identifying the major key represented by any key signature that contains sharps. Find the line or space position that is one half-step higher than the position of the last sharp to the right in the key signature. This position names the major key. As you can see, this pattern is similar in both clefs.

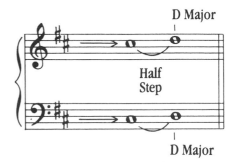

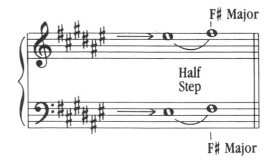

The easiest way to memorize the order of the sharps as they appear in the key signatures is to examine the pattern of sharps in the key of C♯ major, which features all seven sharps.

Take a look at the distance between each consecutive sharp in the key signature of C♯ major. Stepping down the staff by lines and spaces, the second sharp (C♯) is three note positions lower on the staff than the first sharp (F♯). The third sharp (G♯) is four positions higher on the staff than the second sharp (C♯)— and the fourth sharp is three steps lower than the third.

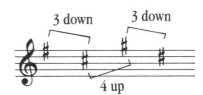

In order to avoid placing the fifth sharp of the pattern (A♯) on a leger line above the staff, this note is moved down an octave to the A♯ which occurs in the second space of the staff. The last two sharps (E♯ and B♯) return to the original pattern.

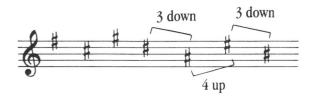

This pattern is identical in bass clef.

F  C  G  D  A  E  B

Familiarize yourself with the pattern of sharps. Practice writing the seven sharps that make up the key signature of C♯ major. Then write in the name of the major key indicated by each of these key signatures.

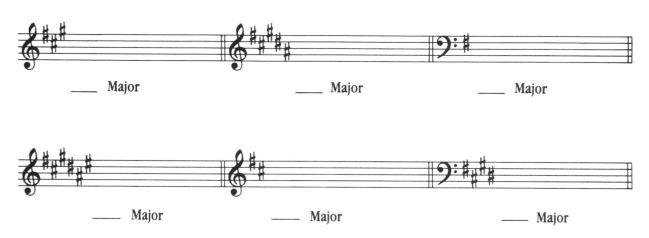

_____ Major          _____ Major          _____ Major

_____ Major          _____ Major          _____ Major

# The Flat Keys

Now let's focus on the key signatures that contain flats. Here's the F major scale, which features one flat.

**F Major Scale**

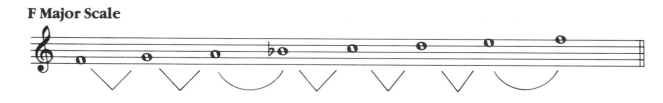

The B♭ major scale features two flats.

**B♭ Major Scale**

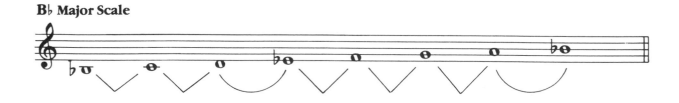

Familiarize yourself with all of the major key signatures and corresponding scales that contain flats.

## The Flat Keys

F Major Scale

B♭ Major Scale

E♭ Major Scale

A♭ Major Scale

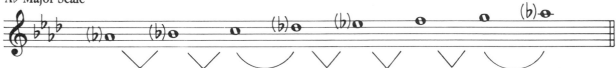

D♭ Major Scale

G♭ Major Scale

C♭ Major Scale

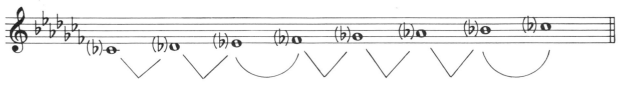

Here's a trick for identifying the major key represented by a key signature with flats. Find the second to the last flat of the key signature. Add a flat to the letter name of that note position and you've got the name of the key. (You'll need to memorize the fact that one flat indicates the key of F major.)

B♭ Major

B♭ Major

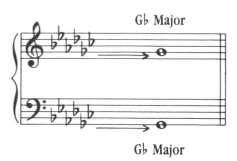

G♭ Major

G♭ Major

To understand the pattern of flats, take a look at the distance between each consecutive flat in the key signature of C♭ major. Stepping up the staff by lines and spaces, the second flat (E♭) is three note positions higher on the staff than the first flat (B♭). The third flat (A♭) is four positions lower on the staff than the second flat (E♭)—the fourth flat is three steps higher than the third, and so on.

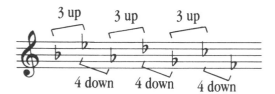

This pattern is the same in bass clef.

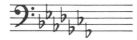

Familiarize yourself with the pattern of flats. Practice writing the seven flats that make up the key signature of C♭ major. Then test your ability to identify the major keys represented by key signatures that contain flats.

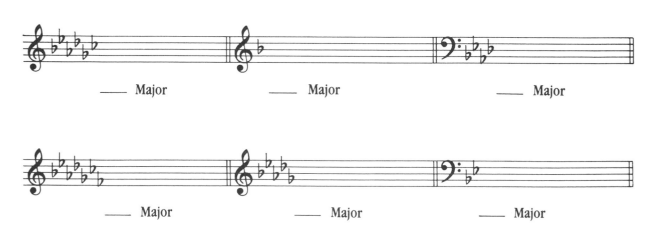

_____ Major          _____ Major          _____ Major

_____ Major          _____ Major          _____ Major

# Compound Time Signatures

You are already familiar with the simple time signatures, like $\frac{3}{4}$ and $\frac{4}{4}$. *Compound time signatures* obey the same rules as simple time signatures, but the rhythmic stresses they create in music are based upon beats that are always counted in multiples of three. The top number of a compound time signature is always a multiple of three to reflect this pattern of stress. Let's look at the most common compound time signature to appear in written music, $\frac{6}{8}$.

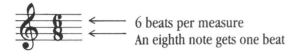

As you can see, there are six beats to the measure, with an eighth note valued at one beat. Notice that a stressed beat occurs every three eighth-note beats, providing two stresses in every measure. This is illustrated by boldface numbers in the first phrase of "The Irish Washerwoman."

**The Irish Washerwoman**

This same counting pattern occurs in music written in $\frac{6}{4}$ and $\frac{6}{16}$.

Time signatures which call for nine beats in a measure also create a stress every three beats. In $\frac{9}{8}$ time, there are three stresses in every measure.

$\frac{12}{8}$ time features twelve beats—and so four stresses—in every measure.

1 2 3 **4** 5 6 7 8 9 **10** 11 12   1 2 3 **4** 5 6 7 8 9 **10** 11 12

As with their "simple" counterparts, $\frac{3}{4}$ and $\frac{4}{4}$ time, the first stress in each measure of $\frac{9}{8}$ and $\frac{12}{8}$ time is generally the strongest. You may sometimes encounter *complex time signatures*—like $\frac{5}{4}$, $\frac{5}{8}$, $\frac{7}{4}$, or $\frac{7}{8}$—which call for unusual numbers of beats in each measure. These time signatures support different patterns of stress. $\frac{5}{4}$ and $\frac{7}{8}$ time are each illustrated below in a typical pattern of stress.

1 2 3 4 5   1 2 3 4 5         1 2 3 4 5 6 7   1 2 3 4 5 6 7

You may find that a time signature changes in the middle of a piece to create an entirely new rhythm. This can be seen in the traditional carol, "Here We Come A-Wassailing." At the beginning of the song's chorus, the timing changes from $\frac{6}{8}$ to $\frac{4}{4}$.

**Here We Come A-Wassailing**

Here we come a - wand - 'ring, so fair ___ to be seen: Love and

joy come to you, And to you your was - sail too,

With a little practice, you should be able to count any new timing correctly. To familiarize yourself with the more commonly used compound time signatures, practice counting and playing these melody phrases.

**Sweet Betsy From Pike**

---

**Boogie Woogie Bugle Boy**

**Barcarolle (from** *Tales of Hoffman*)

**Beautiful Dreamer**

# More About Note Values and Rhythm

By now, you are quite familiar with basic note and rest values. Let's look at some new note values and signs that express information about the rhythm of a piece of music.

## Ties

Some notes are actually made up of two note values which are linked together with a *tie*. A tie indicates that a note be held for the combined length of the two tied notes. For this reason, the two notes that are tied together on the staff always have exactly the same pitch. Ties are often used to link two notes across the barline, as can be seen in the last two bars of this excerpt from "Daisy Bell (A Bicycle Built for Two)."

**Daisy Bell (A Bicycle Built for Two)**

Sometimes tied notes are used within a bar to make the rhythm easy to count within a certain musical context.

Ties may also be used in sequence for this purpose.

If a note altered by an accidental is tied across the barline, the second note is also affected. Any subsequent notes of the same pitch will be unaffected.

Because of their similar appearance, ties are often confused with *slurs,* which are defined in the later section on accents and articulation. The way to tell them apart is to remember that ties link notes of the same pitch, while slurs always link notes of different pitches.

# Extended Rests

Extended rests are used primarily in orchestral or band music since these genres often require that certain instruments rest for several bars. A numeral above the sign indicates the number of measures for which the instruments should rest. This sign indicates that the rest should last for twelve bars.

# Pauses

Sometimes a composer or arranger wishes to indicate that the regular beat or tempo of a piece should hold or pause for a moment on a specific note or rest. This hold or pause is indicated with a *fermata,* as shown in the following two phrases of "For He's a Jolly Good Fellow." (The amount of time which the indicated note or rest should be held is left to the discretion of the performer.)

**For He's a Jolly Good Fellow**

Another kind of pause of indefinite length is indicated with two slashes above the staff (//). This marking is called a *cesura* (or *caesura*)—and indicates that the note is held for its normal time value and then followed by an abrupt pause at the performer's discretion.

# Triplets and Other Note Groupings

Composers and arrangers sometimes need to divide a basic note value into three notes of equal value. These three notes are collectively called a *triplet,* which is indicated by the numeral *3* on the beam.

The "eighth-notes" in the triplet above are each worth one-third of one beat. Try clapping the rhythm of "March of the Wooden Soldiers"—and then play it on the piano, or use the instrument of your choice to play this example.

**March of the Wooden Soldiers (from** *The Nutcracker*)

Other note values may be used in a triplet. Here's an example of "quarter notes" linked in a triplet. Notice that a bracket is used when notes cannot be joined by a beam. Each of these is worth one-third of the value of a half note, or two-thirds of a beat. Play the first phrase of "Hey There, You With the Stars in Your Eyes."

**Hey There, You With the Stars in Your Eyes**

Triplets can also contain dotted notes and rests. Thus, in "Lilliburlero," the dotted "eighth notes" in each triplet are actually worth one-half of a beat. Each "sixteenth note" is worth one-sixth of a beat.

**Lilliburlero**

You may also encounter sixteenth-note triplets or thirty-second-note triplets, as shown in this example.

*Duplets* do not commonly occur in popular music. They are used in music written in compound time signatures to indicate that two notes receive the value commonly afforded to three notes in that timing.

The duplets in this phrase in $\frac{6}{8}$ indicate that the groups of two eighth-notes are played in the time usually allotted to three eighth notes. This means that each note of the duplet is worth one and a half beats in this time signature.

*Quadruplets, quintuplets,* and *sextuplets* are also infrequent.

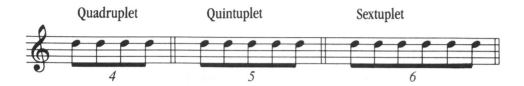

# Tempo

The overall speed of a piece of music is called its *tempo*. Variations in tempo are often used to provide contrast in music, particularly in longer works. Composers and arrangers often indicate approximately how fast a piece should be performed by using an Italian or English term on top of the staff at the beginning of a piece or section. Here are some of the more common Italian tempo markings and their English equivalents.

**Lento** (or **largo**) = Very slow      **Allegretto** = Medium fast
**Adagio** = Slow      **Allegro** = Fast
**Andante** = Walking pace      **Presto** = Very fast
**Moderato** = Medium      **Prestissimo** = As fast as possible

Certain terms call for a changing tempo. The term *rallentando* indicates that the tempo should slow down. *Ritardando* (often abbreviated as *ritard.* or *rit.*) has the same meaning. *Accelerando* calls for a quickening of the tempo. The term *a tempo* tells the musician to return to the normal speed of the piece.

*Tempo commodo* means that the tempo of the piece is left to the discretion of the performer. *Rubato* indicates that the tempo should speed up and slow down according to taste.

## Metronome Markings

The *metronome* is a device that taps out beats of regular intervals. The metronome's speed may be adjusted, and this makes the device useful to musicians for setting regular and precise tempos during practice. Composers and arrangers may indicate a precise tempo by using a *metronome marking* at the beginning of a piece or section. A metronome marking indicates the note value of the basic beat and the number of beats per minute for the piece. This metronome marking tells us that there are sixty quarter-notes per minute—so each quarter note lasts one second. This is a moderately slow tempo (andante).

Compositions with time signatures that call for a half note, dotted quarter, or eighth note to equal one beat may include metronome markings with these notes. Each of the metronome markings that follow represent a moderate tempo (moderato).

Here are some other examples of metronome markings. From left to right they indicate these tempos: adagio, moderato, allegro, and presto.

# Expression

Other Italian and English words are used to indicate that a piece or section be played with a certain expressive quality or feeling. Here are a few of the common Italian and English terms of this kind. Notice that some of these terms also indicate tempo.

**Agitato** = Agitated
**Animato** = Animated
**Appassionato** = With passion
**Bravura** = Boldly
**Brillante** = Brilliantly
**Cantabile** (or **Cantando**) = As if sung
**Con anima** = With feeling
**Con moto** = With movement
**Con spirito** = With spirit
**Dolce** = Sweetly
**Doloroso** = Sorrowfully

**Energico** = Energetically
**Espressivo** = Expressively
**Facile** = Easily
**Grave** = Slow and solemn
**Legato** = Smoothly
**Maestoso** = Majestically
**Mesto** = Sadly
**Scherzando** = Playfully
**Semplice** = Simply
**Sostenuto** = Sustained
**Vivace** = Lively

You will probably encounter other terms of this kind as you continue your study of written music. It's a good idea to have a music dictionary handy during your study and practice time to look up any terms with which you are unfamiliar.

# Dynamics

Volume is another important factor in musical performance. Terms or symbols that indicate volume are called *dynamic markings*. Italian or English words may be used at the beginning of a piece to indicate overall volume. Symbols are often used to abbreviate these words, especially to indicate volume changes during the piece. Take the time to memorize these common dynamic symbols and their corresponding meanings in Italian and English.

*ppp* = **Pianississimo** = As soft as possible

*pp* = **Pianissimo** = Very soft

*p* = **Piano** = Soft

*mp* = **Mezzo piano** = Moderately soft

*mf* = **Mezzo forte** = Moderately loud

*f* = **Forte** = Loud

*ff* = **Fortissimo** = Very loud

*fff* = **Fortississimo** = As loud as possible

Sometimes a composer or arranger wishes to indicate a more gradual change in volume. An increase in volume is indicated by the term *crescendo* (or *cresc.*). The terms *decrescendo* and *diminuendo* (or *dim.*) are used interchangeably to indicate a decrease in volume.

Volume changes may be indicated for specific notes or phrases of a piece by using a *crescendo* or *diminuendo symbol*. A crescendo is traditionally observed in the last four bars of from "For He's a Jolly Good Fellow," as shown in this excerpt. A diminuendo usually occurs after the high note at the end of "O Holy Night." As you can see from these examples, the relative lengths of the lines that form these symbols indicate the notes included in the volume changes.

**For He's a Jolly Good Fellow**

**O Holy Night**

# Structure

In basic terms, an instrumental piece or song should have a clear beginning which leads to the body of the piece (often called the *development section*) and an effective ending. Popular songs often feature an *introduction* or *verse section* as an opener—leading to the *chorus* or main section of the piece. In classical music, there are many different conventions for arranging the individual sections of a work.

Let's take a look at the different markings and symbols that guide the musician through the various sections of a musical composition. Bear in mind that the musical examples used in this section are thumbnail illustrations of the functions of these markings and symbols. In a full-sized musical composition, several pages of music may actually occur between symbols—so it's a good idea to review their placement and meaning before you begin to play or sing a particular piece.

## Repeat Sign

Most styles of music call for their individual sections to be repeated at times. In fact, this kind of repetition is often important to the structure of a musical composition. Two dots before a double bar form a *repeat sign*. If this sign occurs at the end of the piece, it indicates that you should repeat the entire piece once from the beginning. Play "Hot Cross Buns" twice through in tempo.

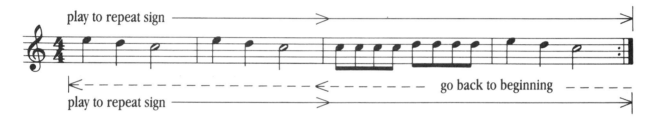

If a repeat sign occurs in the middle of a piece, go back to the beginning and repeat the section before going on.

If a mirror image of the repeat sign occurs earlier in the piece, the performer should only repeat from that point onward. This version of "Hot Cross Buns" has a pickup measure at the beginning. The inverted repeat sign indicates that you should skip this measure when you repeat the piece.

# Repeat Markings: Da Capo and Dal Segno

*D.C.* is an abbreviation of the Italian phrase *Da Capo* (pronounced "dah cahpo"), meaning "from the head." This marking means the same thing as a single repeat sign—repeat the piece from its beginning.

*D.S.* is short for the Italian phrase *Dal Segno* (pronounced "dahl senyo"), meaning "from the sign." *D.S.* means that the performer should go back to the *dal segno sign* (𝄋) and repeat the section.

# Alternate Endings

Sometimes a composer or arranger wants a section repeated with an alternate ending. A bracket and numeral is used in these instances to mark the measure or measures of each different ending. This means that you should skip the *first ending* on the repeat and go on to the *second ending*.

Let's look at how the markings, *Da Capo* and *Dal Segno* may be used to indicate alternate endings. *D.C. al Coda* tells you to repeat the piece until you reach the *coda sign* ( ⊕ )—then skip to the next coda sign, and play or sing the *coda,* which is a short ending section (literally "tail" in Italian).

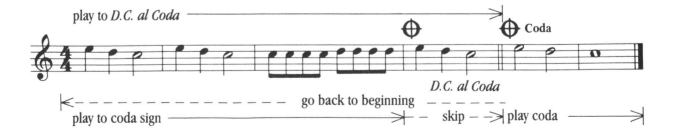

*D.S. al Coda* indicates that you should repeat from the *dal segno* sign. Once you reach the coda sign, skip to the next coda sign, and play or sing the coda section. *D.C. al Coda* and *D.S. al Coda* are sometimes written *D.C. al* ⊕ and *D.S. al* ⊕

*Fine* (pronounced "feenay") is the Italian word for "end." This marking is used in conjunction with repeat markings to indicate the point at which the piece ends. *D.C. al Fine* indicates that you should go back to the beginning of the piece and repeat until you come to the marking *Fine*.

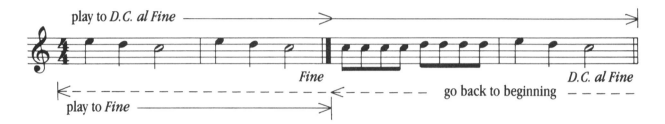

*D.S. al Fine* tells you to go back to the *dal segno* sign and repeat until the point marked *Fine*.

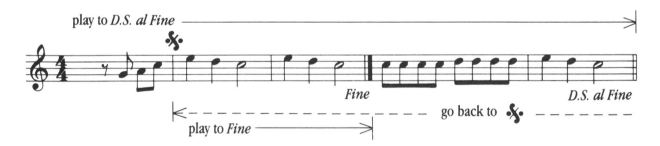

# Accents and Articulations

Different accents and articulations are used to create distinctive phrases or points of interest in a piece.

## Staccato

If a dot appears above or below a note, that note should be played or sung with a short and crisp action called *staccato*. Staccato notes with upward stems feature the staccato marking beneath the notehead. Notes with downward stems feature the dot above the notehead. In order to create a short, sharp sound, a staccato note receives less than half its indicated value. For example, quarter notes with this marking will be approximately equivalent to sixteenth notes.

A triangle above or below a note also indicates that it should be treated as a staccato, though this marking generally calls for somewhat more stress.

## Accents

Notes marked with any of these *accent signs* are to be played or sung with a strong accent and held for their full note value.

The symbols *sf*, *sz*, and *sfz* (short for *sforzando*), as well as *rf* (short for *rinforzando*), indicate that a very strong accent be applied to the designated note.

# Slur

A curved line connecting two or more notes calls for them to be played smoothly. The *slur* should not be confused with the *tie,* which calls for two notes of the same pitch to be played as one note value.

Sometimes a slur is used with staccato markings to indicate that the notes be played halfway between staccato and legato—that is, they are still detached, yet somewhat smooth.

# Phrase Mark

A *phrase mark* is a curved line used by composers and arrangers to indicate the natural punctuation of a musical piece. Phrase marks are usually used to highlight longer passages than slurs, as shown in the first two phrases of "Joy to the World." Notice that a tie also appears in the last measure of this example.

When used in a song, phrase marks often correspond with the natural punctuation of its lyrics. This type of agreement of phrasing between melody and lyrics helps make a song memorable and structurally sound.

# Ornaments

*Ornaments* are musical decorations that provide points of interest in a piece. These appear primarily in the classical music of yesteryear.

## Grace Note

The *grace note* is a small note that adjoins a full-sized note. It is usually depicted as a small eighth note with a slash through its flag and stem. The grace note you will encounter most often in written music is the *unaccented grace note*. This note should be played as quickly as possible just before the natural beat of the note that follows. Here is the grace note, both as it is notated and as it is actually played.

**Unaccented Grace Note**

A grace note that features an accent sign is called an *accented grace note* or *appoggiatura.* This note should be played as quickly as possible on the natural beat of the note that follows. Thus, the value of the grace note is deducted from that of the full-sized note, as shown.

**Accented Grace Note**

Grace notes may also occur in groups. These are usually unaccented grace notes and their time value is deducted from that of the previous beat. A group of two or three grace notes usually features two beams, like sixteenth notes. Groups of four or more grace notes feature three beams, like thirty-second notes. Multiple grace notes should be played quite quickly, according to the skill and taste of the performer.

# Trill

A *trill* is an ornament that consists of the rapid alternation of a note with the note above it. A trill lasts for the full length of the indicated note. Here is a quarter note with a trill, and an illustration of how the trill is actually played.

Longer trills usually include a wavy line after the trill symbol.

# Tremolo

A *tremolo* is indicated by two half notes joined together with a beam. This means that these two pitches should each be played twice in an alternating pattern of eighth notes.

When half notes are joined with a double beam, the two notes are played four times each in an alternating pattern of sixteenth notes. A triple beam indicates that you play eight alternating thirty-second notes—which, in effect, means to play the alternating pattern as quickly as possible. Tremolos may also be applied to other note values as follows.

In music for stringed instruments, the term tremolo is used to indicate the rapid repetition of the same note. This figure is indicated with three slash marks through the note's stem, as shown.

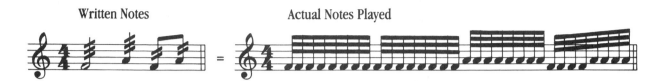

# Turns

A *turn* symbol ( ∾ or ~ ) placed over a note indicates that a certain pattern of notes should be played or sung, as shown.

If a turn symbol is placed after a note, the pattern begins on the second half of the beat.

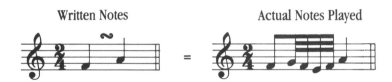

An *inverted turn* is indicated with an inverted turn symbol ( ∾ ) and indicates that the turn begin on the note below the written note, as shown. (An inverted turn may also be indicated with the symbols ~ and ⸇.)

If the inverted turn symbol is placed after a note, the pattern begins on the second half of the beat.

# Mordents

The *mordent* symbol calls for the quick alternation of the written note with the note above it, as shown. The *lower mordent* calls for the alternation of the written note with the note below it. This ornament appears more commonly than the mordent, which is sometimes called the *upper mordent.*

**Upper Mordent**

Written Notes          Actual Notes Played

**Lower Mordent**

Written Notes          Actual Notes Played

# Intervals

The distance between two notes is called an *interval.* To understand how intervals are named, let's look at the *degrees* (or numerical names) of the notes of the C major scale.

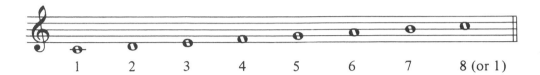

1    2    3    4    5    6    7    8 (or 1)

## Diatonic Intervals

Here are the intervals which correspond to the scale in C major. These are called *diatonic intervals.* Practice playing or singing these intervals until you are familiar with the name and characteristic sound of each one.

Steps:     1          2          2½          3½          4½          5½          6

Name:    Major      Major      Perfect     Perfect      Major       Major      Perfect
         Second     Third      Fourth      Fifth        Sixth       Seventh    Octave

Some intervals move from a low note to a higher note, while others move from high to low. All of these are called *melodic intervals.* Now try playing the notes of each interval backward—that is, from the highest to lowest note.

Perfect     Major       Major       Perfect     Perfect     Major       Major
Octave      Seventh     Sixth       Fifth       Fourth      Third       Second

When the notes of these intervals are played simultaneously, they are called *harmonic intervals.* Listen to the notes of each interval played simultaneously on the piano or guitar.

Major       Major       Perfect     Perfect     Major       Major       Perfect
Second      Third       Fourth      Fifth       Sixth       Seventh     Octave

Intervals may occur on different notes of the scale in different keys. It's easy to identify an interval by its position on the staff. For example:

 An interval of a second always contains one note on a line and one note on an adjacent space.

 An interval of a third always either contains two notes on adjacent lines or two notes on adjacent spaces.

 A fourth always contains a note on a space and a note on a line with one line and one space in between.

 A fifth always contains two notes on spaces with one space skipped, or two notes on lines with one line skipped.

 A sixth always contains one note on a line and one note on a space with two lines and two spaces skipped.

 A seventh always contains two notes on spaces with two spaces skipped, or two notes on lines with two lines skipped.

 An octave always contains one note on a line and one note on a space, with three lines and three spaces skipped.

# Chromatic Intervals

When a diatonic interval is made larger or smaller by an interval of a half step, a *chromatic interval* results. Let's take a look at the now familiar diatonic intervals and their corresponding lowered and raised chromatic intervals in sequence.

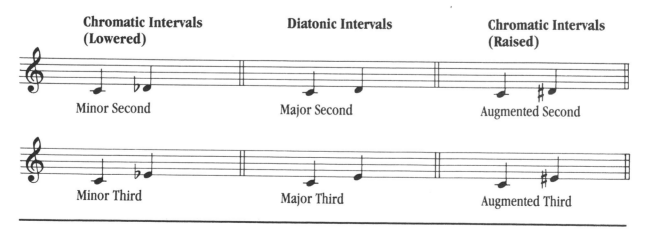

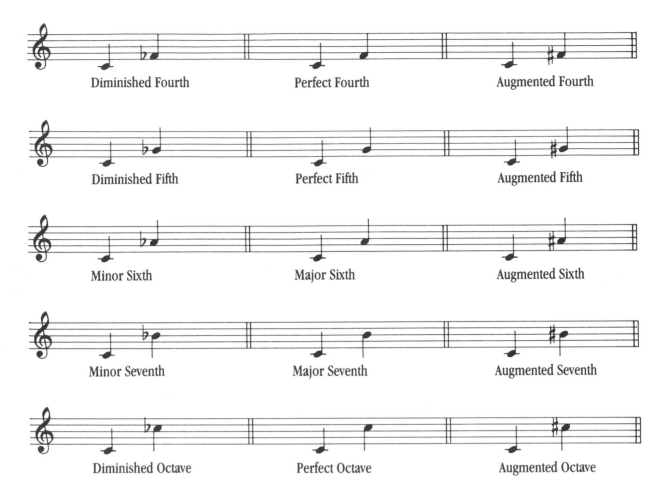

One interval that has not been featured in the preceding charts is the *perfect unison*. The perfect unison may be diminished and augmented like any other perfect interval.

Take the time to memorize the name and appearance of each of the chromatic intervals. Play (or sing and play) each interval backward and forward until you are familiar with its sound. You'll find that certain intervals—like the augmented second and minor third—sound exactly alike. Determine which other intervals sound alike. (These intervals occur in a predictable pattern.)

When naming a chromatic interval, first determine the name of its unaltered form (second, third, fourth, and so on). Then determine the chromatic interval's name by ascertaining whether the diatonic interval has been made larger or smaller by one half-step (according to the major scale of the lower note). Label each of these diatonic and chromatic intervals. Be sure to consider the clef and key signature of each.

Many teachers recommend that you memorize musical intervals by association with their occurrence in famous melodies. Here are some suggested melody phrases to use for this purpose. The indicated interval is shown in brackets. (Notice that the interval of a major seventh, as illustrated in "Bali Hai," is formed between the first and third notes. The perfect fifth occurs between the second and third notes of "Twinkle, Twinkle, Little Star.") The common abbreviation for each interval is also included above the bracket. It's a good idea to commit these abbreviations to memory as well. You should feel free to come up with other melody phrases to use when memorizing these intervals.

Give yourself some more practice at identifying intervals by examining other music and labelling each interval of the melody. The study and practice of intervals is an important listening skill. The mastery of this skill is central to a musician's ability to sightread written music. You may find it useful and fun to get together with a friend for cooperative study of this subject—and take turns playing, singing, and identifying intervals together.

# Double Sharps and Double Flats

Though they rarely occur, you may come across a *double sharp* or *double flat* in written music. These accidentals are seldom necessary—and keys that may require their use are generally avoided. However, double sharps or double flats are sometimes used to maintain a logical pattern of notes on the staff.

A *double sharp* (×) raises the indicated note by two half-steps. If the note is already sharped in the key signature, or by a previous accidental in the same measure, the double sharp raises the pitch by one half-step only. In other words, a double sharp raises any note two half-steps from its natural position. Thus, F× is another name for the G note. An F× note is used in the following example to preserve the visual pattern of ascending thirds in the key of E major.

If a G note were used instead of F× in this passage, the pattern of thirds would be violated, and thus more difficult to read.

Sometimes a *natural sharp* sign is used to return a double sharp note to a sharped note in the same measure. However, most authorities agree that the natural sign is superfluous, and a sharp sign alone will suffice, as shown at right.

You may also sometimes see a *double natural* employed to cancel a double sharp completely in the same measure. However, a single natural is quite sufficient for this purpose, as shown at right.

A *double flat* sign lowers the indicated note by two half steps. Here, B♭♭ is used to preserve the pattern of descending thirds in the key of E♭ major.

A *natural flat* sign or *double natural* may occur in some printed music, but the single flat or natural sign is preferable for the partial or complete cancellation of a double flat, as shown at right.

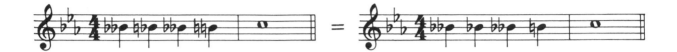

# Minor Key Signatures and Scales

As you know, music may be written in different keys to accommodate the ranges of particular voices or instruments. Another reason for writing a piece in a particular key is to lend a special tonal color, or *tonality,* to a piece. Many of the musical excerpts you have studied in this book so far have been written in a major key, and therefore have major tonalities. Sometimes a composer chooses to use a *minor key* to lend an introspective or sad quality to a piece. This section explores the different minor keys and how they are formed.

There are three forms of the minor scale: the *natural minor,* the *melodic minor,* and the *harmonic minor.* Let's compare the familiar C major scale with these three minor forms. Since all C minor scales use the same starting note as the key of C major, each are called the *tonic minor* of this major key. For this same reason, C major and C minor are also sometimes called *parallel keys.*

C Major Scale

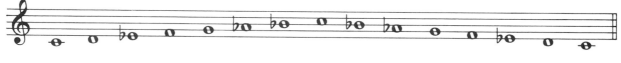

C Natural Minor Scale

C Melodic Minor Scale

C Harmonic Minor Scale

Notice that the third, sixth, and seventh notes (or *degrees*) of the natural minor scale are lowered by one half-step. The melodic minor features a lowered third on the way up the scale, and a lowered third, sixth, and seventh on the way down. The third and sixth of the harmonic minor scale are lowered by one half-step, whether ascending or descending.

In order to avoid the routine writing of the accidentals necessary to create these minor forms, music written in the key of C minor features a key signature with three flats (like the key of E♭ major). This brings the need for accidentals to a minimum. In this key signature, an accidental is required only on the sixth and seventh degrees of the ascending C melodic minor scale—and on the seventh degree of the C harmonic minor scale.

C Melodic Minor Scale

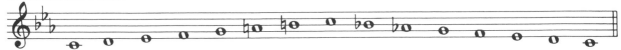

C Harmonic Minor Scale

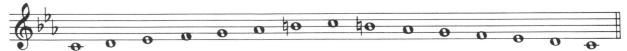

Because the key of C minor uses the same key signature as E♭ major, it is known as the *relative minor* of this major key. Correspondingly, the key of E♭ major is known as the *relative major* of C minor. Presented below are all the harmonic and melodic scale forms in every minor key. The name of each relative major key is shown in parentheses. Notice that the relative major key is always three half-steps (a minor third) up from the note named by the corresponding minor key. Take the time to practice playing or singing each of these minor scales until they become quite familiar.

**Key of A Minor (Relative Minor of C Major)**

A Melodic Minor Scale

A Harmonic Minor Scale

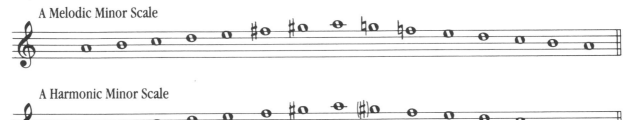

**Key of E Minor (Relative Minor of G Major)**

E Melodic Minor Scale

E Harmonic Minor Scale

**Key of B Minor (Relative Minor of D Major)**

B Melodic Minor Scale

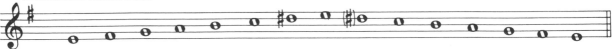

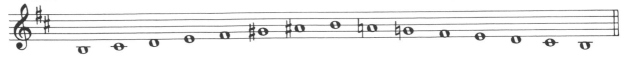

### B Harmonic Minor Scale

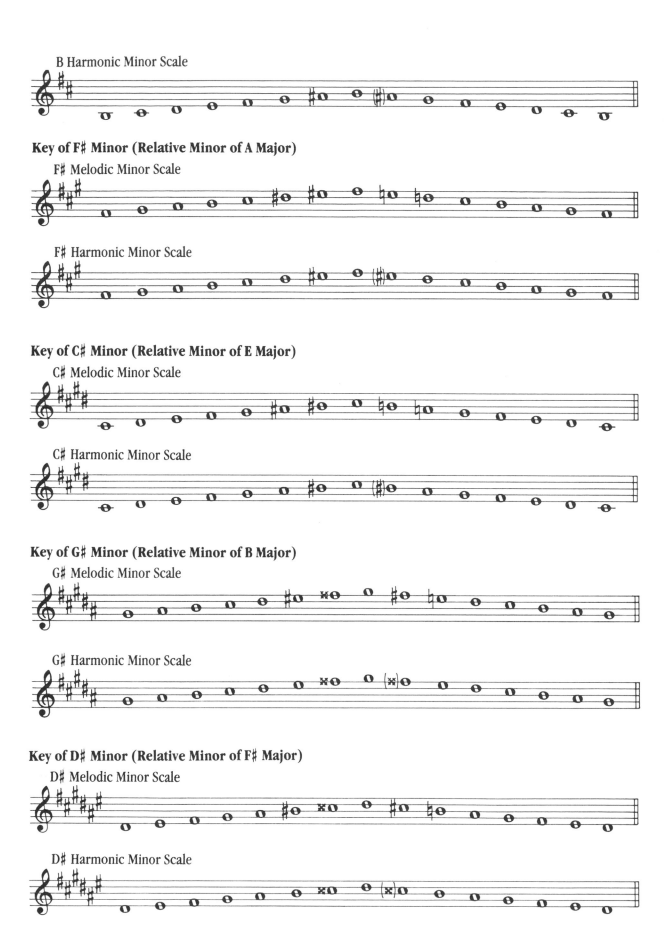

## Key of F# Minor (Relative Minor of A Major)

### F# Melodic Minor Scale

### F# Harmonic Minor Scale

## Key of C# Minor (Relative Minor of E Major)

### C# Melodic Minor Scale

### C# Harmonic Minor Scale

## Key of G# Minor (Relative Minor of B Major)

### G# Melodic Minor Scale

### G# Harmonic Minor Scale

## Key of D# Minor (Relative Minor of F# Major)

### D# Melodic Minor Scale

### D# Harmonic Minor Scale

### Key of A♯ Minor (Relative Minor of C♯ Major)

A♯ Melodic Minor Scale

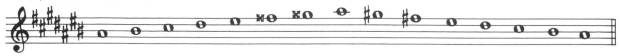

A♯ Harmonic Minor Scale

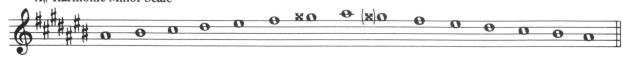

### Key of D Minor (Relative Minor of F Major)

D Melodic Minor Scale

D Harmonic Minor Scale

### Key of G Minor (Relative Minor of B♭ Major)

G Melodic Minor Scale

G Harmonic Minor Scale

### Key of C Minor (Relative Minor of E♭ Major)

C Melodic Minor Scale

C Harmonic Minor Scale

### Key of F Minor (Relative Minor of A♭ Major)

F Melodic Minor Scale

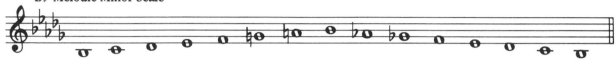

F Harmonic Minor Scale

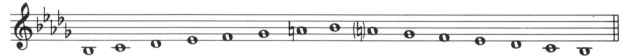

### Key of B♭ Minor (Relative Minor of D♭ Major)

B♭ Melodic Minor Scale

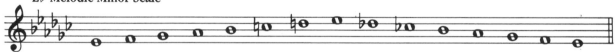

B♭ Harmonic Minor Scale

### Key of E♭ Minor (Relative Minor of G♭ Major)

E♭ Melodic Minor Scale

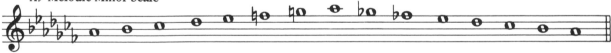

E♭ Harmonic Minor Scale

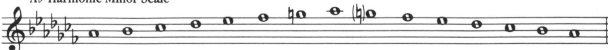

### Key of A♭ Minor (Relative Minor of C♭ Major)

A♭ Melodic Minor Scale

A♭ Harmonic Minor Scale

# Introduction to Chords

As you know, certain instruments—notably the piano, organ, and guitar—are capable of playing more than one note at a time. Three notes played simultaneously produce a *triad,* which is the simplest form of *chord.* (Remember that two notes sounded together would be designated as an *interval.*) An ensemble of instruments or voices may also produce chords, with each member responsible for one or more of the chord tones. Understanding and playing the basic chords that follow will help to deepen your understanding of music as well as develop your musical "ear."

## Major Chord

Let's take a look at some basic chord forms based on the note C. The *C major triad,* or *C major chord,* is formed by taking the first (or *root*), third, and fifth degrees of the C major scale. The abbreviation for this chord—its *chord symbol*—is *C.*

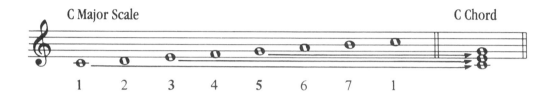

Here are several ways to play a C chord on piano and guitar. Notice the different ways in which the first, third, and fifth may be rearranged and doubled.

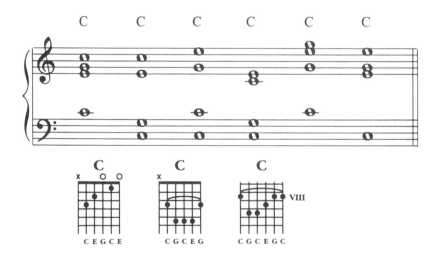

# Inversions

When the lowest note of a chord is not the root, the chord is called an *inversion.* The note that is on the bottom is said to be "in the bass." When the third is in the bass, the chord is said to be "in first inversion."

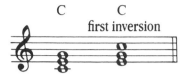

When the fifth is in the bass, the chord is said to be "in second inversion."

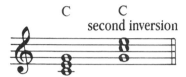

Sometimes a chord symbol will indicate what note is to be placed in the bass. This is done by separating the chord name and the name of the bass note with a slash. Thus, "C, first inversion" becomes "C/E" and "C, second inversion" becomes "C/G."

# Seventh Chord

A *C7 chord* (pronounced "C seven") is formed by simply adding a flatted seventh to the C triad.

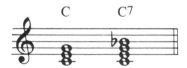

Here are several ways to play the C7 chord, including a few inversions.

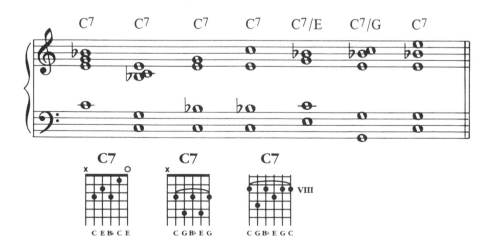

# Minor Chord

If you lower the third of a C major chord by one half-step, you get a *C minor chord.* The C minor chord is abbreviated *Cm.*

As with any chord, there are many ways to play Cm. Here are a few good voicings.

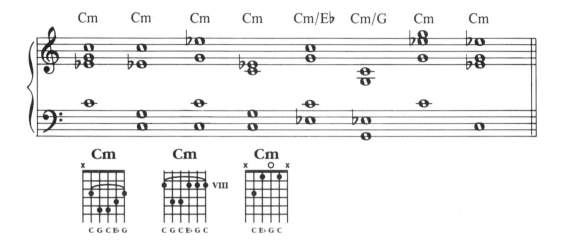

# Minor Seventh Chord

Add the flatted seventh to the C minor chord and the *C minor seventh chord* results. This chord is abbreviated *Cm7.*

Try playing these forms of the C minor seventh chord.

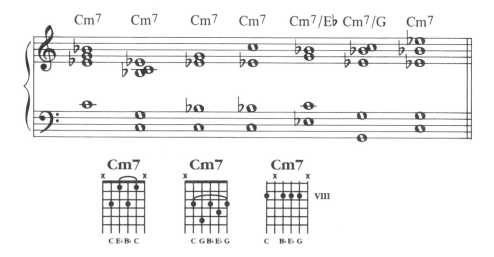

# Augmented and Diminished Chords

An *augmented chord* is a major triad with a sharped fifth. The abbreviation for an augmented chord is a plus sign ( + ) or *aug*. A *diminished chord* is formed by flatting the fifth of a minor chord and is abbreviated with the degree sign (°) or *dim*.

Diminished chords are usually embellished by the addition of the double-flatted seventh (°7).

# Major Sixth and Major Seventh Chords

*Major sixth* and *major seventh chords* are often used in place of regular major chords. They are formed by adding the sixth or seventh degree, respectively, to a major triad. The symbol for a major sixth chord is simply the numeral *6*. A major seventh chord is indicated by the symbol *maj7* or *M7*.

# Basic Chords in All Keys

So far, we've looked at eight important chords forms: major, minor, seventh, minor seventh, augmented, diminished, major sixth, and major seventh. Each of these chord forms may be adapted to any key by selecting the appropriate notes from the corresponding major scale. For example, to form a G major chord, take the first, third, and fifth degrees of the G major scale: G, B, D; to produce a D minor chord take the first, third, and fifth of the D major scale (D, F♯, A) and flat the third, yielding D, F, A.

Here is a chart of each of the chord forms you have learned, as notated for piano. For guitarists, a corresponding chart of these chords is also provided. Try playing each of these chords in every key on one of these instruments.

**Basic Chords in All Keys for Piano**

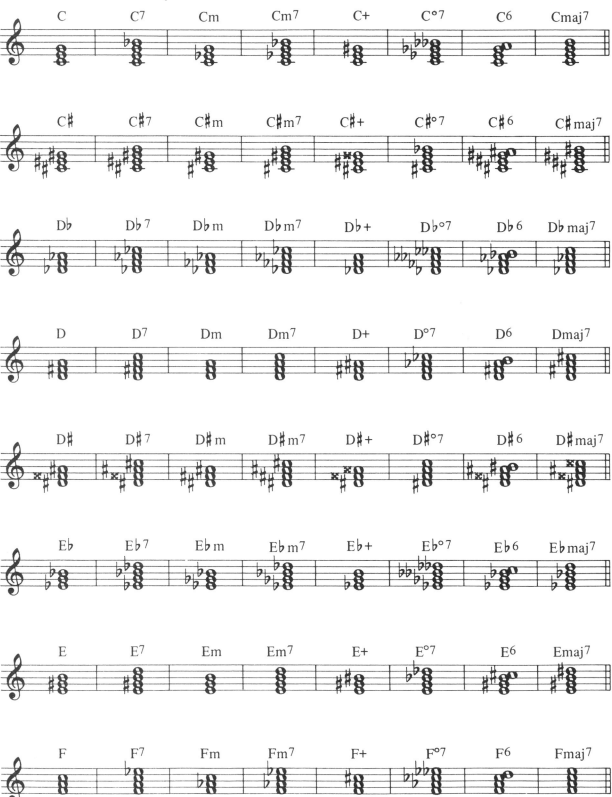

## Basic Chords in All Keys for Guitar

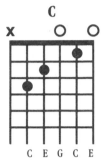

C

C E G C E

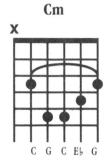

C7

C E B♭ C E

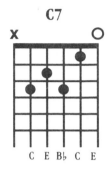

Cm

C G C E♭ G

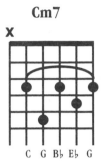

Cm7

C G B♭ E♭ G

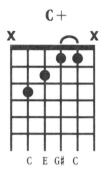

C+

C E G♯ C

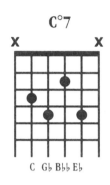

C°7

C G♭ B♭♭ E♭

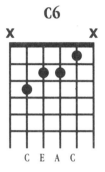

C6

C E A C

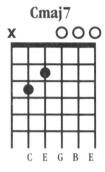

Cmaj7

C E G B E

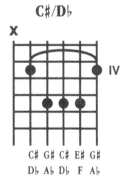

C♯/D♭

C♯ G♯ C♯ E♯ G♯
D♭ A♭ D♭ F A♭

IV

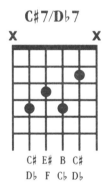

C♯7/D♭7

C♯ E♯ B C♯
D♭ F C♭ D♭

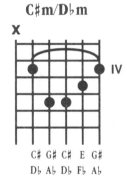

C♯m/D♭m

C♯ G♯ C♯ E G♯
D♭ A♭ D♭ F♭ A♭

IV

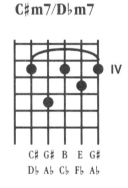

C♯m7/D♭m7

C♯ G♯ B E G♯
D♭ A♭ C♭ F♭ A♭

IV

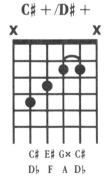

C♯+/D♯+

C♯ E♯ G× C♯
D♭ F A D♭

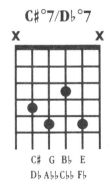

C♯°7/D♭°7

C♯ G B♭ E
D♭ A♭♭ C♭♭ F♭

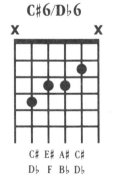

C♯6/D♭6

C♯ E♯ A♯ C♯
D♭ F B♭ D♭

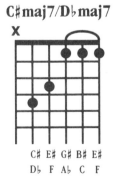

C♯maj7/D♭maj7

C♯ E♯ G♯ B♯ E♯
D♭ F A♭ C F

**D**

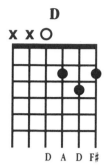

D A D F#

**D7**

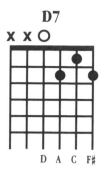

D A C F#

**Dm**

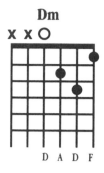

D A D F

**Dm7**

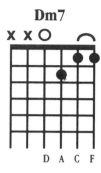

D A C F

**D+**

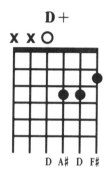

D A# D F#

**D°7**

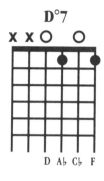

D Ab Cb F

**D6**

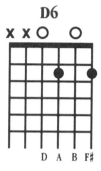

D A B F#

**Dmaj7**

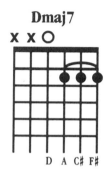

D A C# F#

**D#/Eb**

D# A# D# Fx
Eb Bb Eb G

**D#7/Eb7**

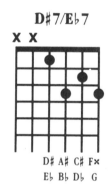

D# A# C# Fx
Eb Bb Db G

**D#m/Ebm**

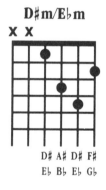

D# A# D# F#
Eb Bb Eb Gb

**D#m7/Ebm7**

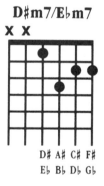

D# A# C# F#
Eb Bb Db Gb

**D#+/Eb+**

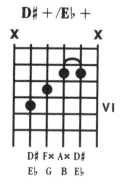

VI

D# Fx Ax D#
Eb G B Eb

**D#°7/Eb°7**

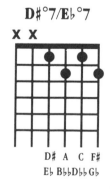

D# A C F#
Eb Bbb Dbb Gb

**D#6/Eb6**

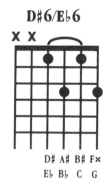

D# A# B# Fx
Eb Bb C G

**D#maj7/Ebmaj7**

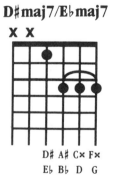

D# A# Cx Fx
Eb Bb D G

**E**

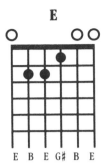

E B E G♯ B E

**E7**

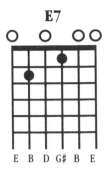

E B D G♯ B E

**Em**

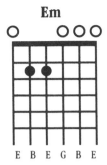

E B E G B E

**Em7**

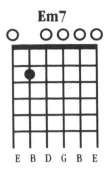

E B D G B E

**E+**

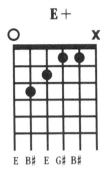

E B♯ E G♯ B♯

**E°7**

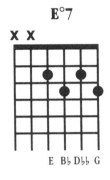

E B♭ D♭♭ G

**E6**

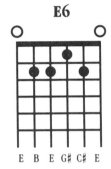

E B E G♯ C♯ E

**Emaj7**

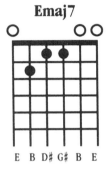

E B D♯ G♯ B E

**F**

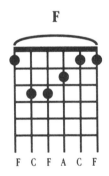

F C F A C F

**F7**

F C E♭ A C F

**Fm**

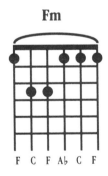

F C F A♭ C F

**Fm7**

F C E♭ A♭ C F

**F+**

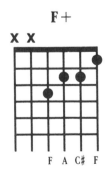

F A C♯ F

**F°7**

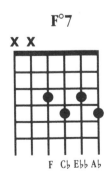

F C♭ E♭♭ A♭

**F6**

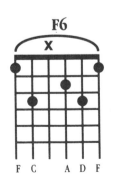

F C A D F

**Fmaj7**

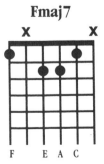

F E A C

### F♯/G♭

F♯ C♯ F♯ A♯ C♯ F♯
G♭ D♭ G♭ B♭ D♭ G♭

### F♯7/G♭7

F♯ C♯ E A♯ C♯ F♯
G♭ D♭ F♭ B♭ D♭ G♭

### F♯m/G♭m

F♯ C♯ F♯ A C♯ F♯
G♭ D♭ G♭ B♭♭ D♭ G♭

### F♯m7/G♭m7

F♯ C♯ E A C♯ F♯
G♭ D♭ F♭ B♭♭ D♭ G♭

### F♯ +/G♭ +
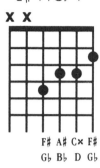

F♯ A♯ C✕ F♯
G♭ B♭ D G♭

### F♯°7/G♭°7
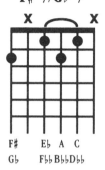

F♯ E♭ A C
G♭ F♭♭ B♭♭ D♭♭

### F♯6/G♭6
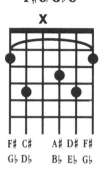

F♯ C♯ A♯ D♯ F♯
G♭ D♭ B♭ E♭ G♭

### F♯maj7/G♭maj7
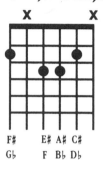

F♯ E♯ A♯ C♯
G♭ F B♭ D♭

### G
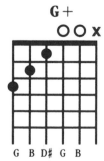

G B D G B G

### G7
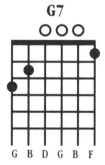

G B D G B F

### Gm
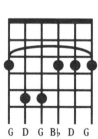

G D G B♭ D G

### Gm7
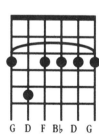

G D F B♭ D G

### G +
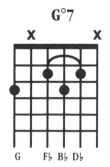

G B D♯ G B

### G°7
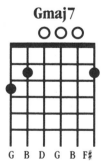

G F♭ B♭♭ D♭♭

### G6
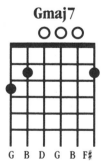

G B D G B E

### Gmaj7

G B D G B F♯

## G#/A♭
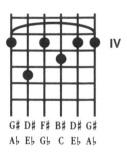
IV

G# D# G# B# D# G#
A♭ E♭ A♭ C E♭ A♭

## G#7/A♭7
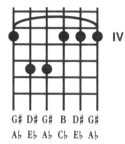
IV

G# D# F# B# D# G#
A♭ E♭ G♭ C E♭ A♭

## G#m/A♭m
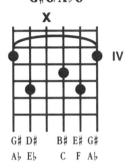
IV

G# D# G# B D# G#
A♭ E♭ A♭ C♭ E♭ A♭

## G#m7/A♭m7
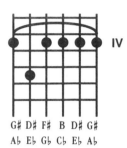
IV

G# D# F# B D# G#
A♭ E♭ G♭ C♭ E♭ A♭

## G# + /A♭ +
X X
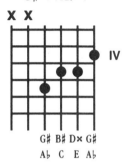
IV

G# B# D✕ G#
A♭ C E A♭

## G#°7/A♭°7
X X
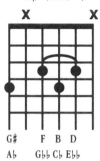

G# F B D
A♭ G♭♭ C♭ E♭♭

## G#6/A♭6
X
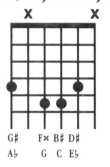
IV

G# D# B# E# G#
A♭ E♭ C F A♭

## G#maj7/A♭maj7
X X
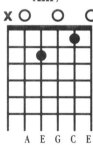

G# F✕ B# D#
A♭ G C E♭

## A
X O O
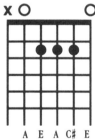

A E A C# E

## A7
X O O O
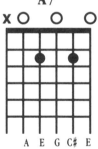

A E G C# E

## Am
X O O
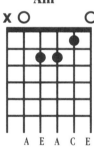

A E A C E

## Am7
X O O O
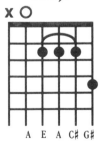

A E G C E

## A +
X O
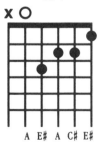

A E# A C# E#

## A°7
X O
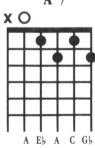

A E♭ A C G♭

## A6
X O
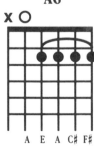

A E A C# F#

## Amaj7
X O
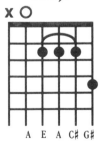

A E A C# G#

## A#/Bb

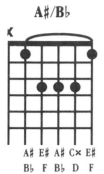

A# E# A# C× E#
Bb F Bb D F

## A#7/Bb7

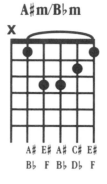

A# E# G# C× E#
Bb F Ab D F

## A#m/Bbm

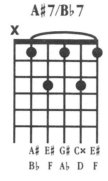

A# E# A# C# E#
Bb F Bb Db F

## A#m7/Bbm7

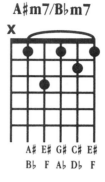

A# E# G# C# E#
Bb F Ab Db F

## A#+/Bb+

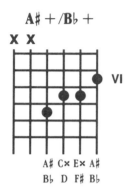

VI

A# C× E× A#
Bb D F# Bb

## A#°7/Bb°7

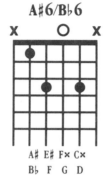

A# E G C# E
Bb Fb Abb Db Fb

## A#6/Bb6

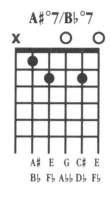

A# E# F× C×
Bb F G D

## A#maj7/Bbmaj7

A# E# G× C× E#
Bb F A D F

## B

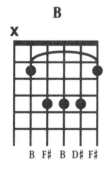

B F# B D# F#

## B7

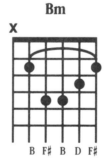

B D# A B F#

## Bm

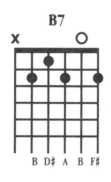

B F# B D F#

## Bm7

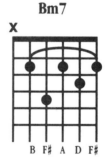

B F# A D F#

## B+

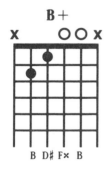

B D# F× B

## B°7

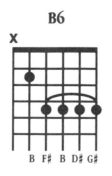

B F Ab D

## B6

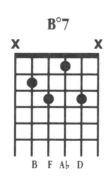

B F# B D# G#

## Bmaj7

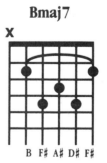

B F# A# D# F#

# Reading a Lead Sheet

A *lead sheet* is a printed version of a song which contains the melody and chord symbols (and sometimes the lyrics). Now that you are familiar with the basic chords in all keys, try playing a lead sheet of the song "Aura Lee," which provided the melody for the Elvis Presley hit "Love Me Tender." This song contains many of the chords you have just learned. If you need to be reminded of the fingering of any chord, simply refer to the previous chord charts. Pianists should play the melody with the right hand and the chords with the left hand. If you are a guitarist, strum the chords as indicated—and hum along if you like.

# Transposing Chords

In order to make a particular song lower or higher in pitch, you must *transpose* it to a different key. Once you know the chords to a song, it's easy to transpose it to any key you wish.

The most commonly used chords in any major key are the major chords built on the first, fourth, and fifth degrees of the scale. These are often referred to as *I, IV, and V7 chords*. If you know the I, IV, and V7 chords in every key, then you know the chords to thousands of songs. Here is a chart of these chords for quick reference.

| I | IV | V7 | | I | IV | V7 |
|---|----|----|---|---|----|----|
| C | F | G7 | | G♭ | C♭ | D♭ 7 |
| C♯ | F♯ | G♯ 7 | | G | C | D7 |
| D♭ | G♭ | A♭ 7 | | A♭ | D♭ | E♭ 7 |
| D | G | A7 | | A | D | E7 |
| E♭ | A♭ | B♭ 7 | | B♭ | E♭ | F7 |
| E | A | B7 | | B | E | F♯ 7 |
| F | B♭ | C7 | | C♭ | F♭ | G♭ 7 |
| F♯ | B | C♯ 7 | | | | |

Try playing the song "Danny Boy" in the key of C (using the C, F, and G7 chords, as shown in the previous chart). Once you are familiar with playing the song in this key, refer to the chart and play "Danny Boy" in other keys.

**Danny Boy**

## Further Chord Study

Take the time to explore reading and playing the chords and melody of your favorite songs, as well as ones that are unfamiliar to you. You'll find hours of enjoyment reading through sheet music and song collections as you strengthen these important reading skills. In fact, if you play the guitar or piano, you should obtain a complete chord fingering chart for your instrument. You may also wish to pursue an in-depth study of chord forms and structure, as is provided in any good music theory textbook. This further study is also advisable for those who wish to compose or arrange music.

A basic understanding of the more advanced theoretical aspects of written music can only serve to enhance your music reading skills. However, at this point, you have all the facts you need to be a knowledgable and competent reader. The music store and music library will provide you with many new doorways to a lifetime of reading enjoyment.

# Answers to Written Exercises

**Page**

4  "Yankee Doodle"
CCDE | CEDG | CCDE | CB | CCDE | FEDC | BGAB | CC | ABAG | ABC | GAGF | EG | ABAG | ABCA | GCBD | CC ‖

"Aura Lee *(Love Me Tender)*"
GCBC | DAD | CBAB | C | |

5  "Surprise Symphony"
CCEE | GGE | FFDD | BBG | |

"Angels We Have Heard on High"
BBBD | DCB | BABD | BAG | |

"Scarborough Fair"
DD | AAA | EFE | D | |

6  "Twinkle, Twinkle, Little Star"
CCGG | AAG | |

"My Bonnie"
G | EDC | DCA | GE | |

8  "Danny Boy *(Londonderry Air)*"
BCD | ED | EAGE | DCA | CEF | GA | GECE | D | GCD | ED | EAGE | DCA | BCD | EF | EDCD | C | |

9    "Hark! the Herald Angels Sing"
GCCB | CEED | GGGF | EDE | |

"Westminster Chimes"
BG | AD | DA | BG | |

"The Ashgrove"
G | CEGF | ECC | DFEDC | BGGG | CEDCB | AFA | GCB | C | |

13    "Old MacDonald"
CCCG | AAG | |

"Camptown Races"
GGEG | AGE | |

"The Streets of Laredo"
G | GFE | FGF | EDC | BG | |

"Good King Wenceslas"
CCCD | CCG | |

14    "The Band Played On"
CEC | BEB | ACA | G | |

"Jesu, Joy of Man's Desiring"
CD | EGF | FAG | GCB | C | |

29    "Show Me the Way to Go Home"
EEE♭EE♭E | CC | FFFFCDE♭ | E | |

"Für Elise"
ED♯ | ED♯EBDC | ACEA | BEG♯B | C | |

"Shine On Harvest Moon"
FE | FEC♯A | F♯FF♯E | D | |

"I Don't Want to Walk Without You, Baby"
AA♭AA♯ | BAFD | A | B | |

34    A Major | | B Major | | G Major | | F♯ Major | | D Major | | E Major | |

36    G♭ Major | | F Major | | A♭ Major | | C♭ Major | | D♭ Major | | B♭ Major | |

59    *Line 1:* Augmented Unison | | Minor Second | | Major Second | | Augmented Second | |
*Line 2:* Major Third | | Minor Third | | Augmented Third | | Major Third | |
*Line 3:* Perfect Fourth | | Augmented Fourth | | Perfect Fourth | | Diminished Fourth | |
*Line 4:* Augmented Fifth | | Perfect Fifth | | Diminished Fifth | | Perfect Fifth | |
*Line 5:* Major Sixth | | Minor Sixth | | Augmented Sixth | | Major Sixth | |
*Line 6:* Major Seventh | | Major Seventh | | Augmented Seventh | | Minor Seventh | |
*Line 7:* Perfect Octave | | Perfect Octave | | Diminished Octave | | Augmented Octave | |